# Talking Blues – Off the Record

Compiled by John Stix

Interviews by John Stix

ISBN: 9798460127221

# INTRODUCTION

When I started writing about music, it was mostly for a jazz audience. My first piece was on Stanley Clarke followed by Airto Moreira and Flora Purim. You guessed it, my big break as a writer came from working with the musicians in the original Return to Forever. Then I spoke with Roland Kirk, Keith Jarrett, Earl "Fatha" Hines and Ron Carter.

Always a fan of *Downbeat* magazine's "Blindfold Test," I adopted this technique of playing other people's music for musicians as a way to get them to talk about themselves. This, I found, also worked very well with rock musicians. The first song I played for an artist would often be something from their youth, their beginning steps as a player. Jethro Tull's Ian Anderson was so excited because he had not heard Roland Kirk's "Serenade to a Cuckoo" in decades. Of course, he went on about how he first learned the flute. When our conversation on that subject came to its natural close, I would play another song, hoping that too would spark a different conversation. And so it went on for years that I used this method to learn about musicians and the songs we listened to together. The first time I put them into a column, it was called "A Good Hard Listen," which appeared in *International Musician and Recording World* magazine. For a decade I called it "In the Listening Room" in *Guitar for the Practicing Musician.*

Over the years I've interviewed many artists several times. And each time I used listening to music to jump start the conversation.

Recently I realized that I had several of these reviews that had never seen the light of day. I thought it would be a good "bathroom read" if I compiled these reviews, most of which did not appear in GFPM. And because it was to be a book, and not confined to the length of a column, I could also go a bit deeper into their thoughts and answers on the music in question.

The middle bars (IV chord) of this book I call Talking Blues. These are excerpts from conversations I had with blues artists beyond the "Off the Record" context. The turnaround of this project is a list of albums the musicians talked about that were either an important part of their listening history or that they intended to buy in the near future.

I hope you enjoy these Talking Blues and Off the Record comments from the musicians you like about the blues music you love.

Be Goode,
John Stix

# CONTENTS

# PART 1: OFF THE RECORD

# PAUL BARRERE (LITTLE FEAT)

**"You've Been in Love Too Long"**
Bonnie Raitt
*Takin' My Time*
**PAUL:** It's a great song. It's not my very favorite Bonnie cut. She has done so many great songs and had so many great players playing on her records. This is a good one. For me though, the thing I don't like about it, was that it was almost too pop. Since that time she has become even more pop, with a better recording of that style of music. But when I first met Bonnie and first saw her play, she was so raw. She did her blues stuff, her Sippie Wallace stuff and then she would do a song like Eric Kaz's "Love Has No Pride," that would tear your heart out. She was also ripping up songs like "Willya Wontcha," the Johnny Lee [Schell] song that she did.

**"Victims of Comfort"**
Keb' Mo'
*Keb' Mo'*
**PAUL:** I don't know his record. As a matter of fact I am going to go out and buy this record. Is this from his first one? My guitar tech told me to get number one as opposed to number two. We did a gig with him in Chicago, and he is almost like the second coming of Taj [Mahal]. He is great. A very personable man. Very nice. I didn't get a whole lot of time to talk to him but I get the feeling he

is from the south somewhere.

**JOHN:** Compton.

**PAUL:** Compton, California. Hell, he was talking about Texas like he was from there. Great. To me, anybody who wants to play traditional blues is okay in my book. He is absolutely real. He also makes it sound contemporary.

**"Rollin' Stone"**

Paul Rodgers (w/ Jeff Beck)

*Muddy Water Blues: A Tribute to Muddy Waters*

**PAUL:** Is it Robben Ford? It's not Robben Ford. Is it Paul Rodgers? Great song. Muddy Waters. It reminds me a lot of how some of the old English bands, Led Zeppelin and so forth, would take a great old blues song and do an updated version of it, which I am always all in favor of. I don't find this offending in any way, shape or form. Whoever is playing guitar has a lot of licks, a lot of chops. He is playing a lot of the same chops that you hear, but he has some great sounds and he's got some good feel to it. It's not something that I would probably gravitate towards on my own. Maybe I would back when I was a kid and listening to Zeppelin. Now I would just as soon put on Muddy's version of it.

**JOHN:** The guitarist was Jeff Beck.

**PAUL:** Wow! Okay. There you go. Jeff Beck is a great guitar player. Some of the stuff that I heard him do more on the fusion level, where it was really Jeff Beck's licks, I liked more. Here you are hearing the same mistake all guitar players make. You take the initial B.B. King licks, Albert King Licks, Freddie King licks and you do them in your own way. And we all do it. We are all guilty, because how many blues licks are there that are original? Stevie Ray was great at it. Eric just made that blues record and in essence is note for note Freddy King. In a strange way I have kind of grown out of that situation. Now I would just as soon put on the old records and listen to them.

**JOHN:** Is there something less subtle in the British blues?

**PAUL:** It has that big amp, big drums, big change over of something that is very classically a blues song. I remember seeing Peter Green play with the Bluesbreakers at the Shrine Auditorium and being absolutely enthralled with how he would perform, and he was as guilty as the rest of us at playing those same King family licks. But he imparted through it part of his own soul. It's a shame the cat's not still playing. I think British blues is great, but you almost get into that Nigel Tufnel, Spinal Tap kind of look when you hear that stuff. You see those guys sneering, "God, this is hurting so bad, I have the blues." I don't get it. I don't feel it. Then you see Taj Mahal or Keb' Mo' and you go, Wow, this is great.

**"Evidence"**
Thelonious Monk
*Straight No Chaser – Original Motion Picture Soundtrack*
**PAUL:** Monk with Charlie Rouse. Once again, it was a very fortunate thing that I had two older brothers and my oldest brother was way off into jazz. So at the age of 13 or 14 I got a really good dose of Thelonious, John Coltrane, Miles Davis. The thing about Thelonious, which I absolutely love, is his style of syncopation, his style of melody, his style of dissonance. When you listen to his comp chords in the background, you immediately know this is Thelonious Monk. His rhythm was unique. It was very influential in how I approach the guitar. There were so many cats that played with Miles and the real educated ear will know if it's Herbie Hancock, or any of those cats. But Monk is a wonder. It's like Mose Allison, who is another cat whose song stylings and playing are special.

## REB BEACH (WINGER, WHITESNAKE)

**"I Can't Turn You Loose"**
The Gadd Gang
*Here and Now*
**REB:** I really hate this. Don't hate me, but it's really boring. Maybe it's B.B. King? But if you want to hear blues I really like, it's Eric Clapton. I don't even have Eric Clapton records. This is really boring music to me. It sounded like elevator music. This is the song from *The Blues Brothers.* See ya. I don't see any fire in that playing. When I see B.B. King on television all the time there is some fire there. When that guy wiggles that note it didn't sound like that guy meant it to me. No offense to whoever he is.

**"The Shakes"**
Blues Saraceno
*Never Look Back*
**REB:** That's it! You hear that and you say, Holy shit! Just from the first note you say, Yeah, and your head starts moving and your eyebrows start rising and you go, Wow, that's something! Blues Saraceno is awesome. He makes you raise an eyebrow. As a guitar player, I could listen to him all day. Randy Coven sounds really good. His bass playing is firmly in the pocket. It's the feel in the guitar playing. It's total feel. Not many guitar players can do that. Someone else can play all those notes and it could just sound terrible. That whole song is great. It's got a groove. It doesn't need a

hook because the playing is so excellent, so melodic. It makes you move.

# JEFF BECK

**"Hoochie Coochie Man"**
Muddy Waters
*The Best of Muddy Waters*
**JEFF:** That song has the building blocks for about a million bands. It's so easy to play—but is it? Try to get that lurch. Nobody phrases like him. They can't. There have been others, but it's the full-bodied hippo voice that he's got. This song had an impact on me, but then, that was the whole applecart being upset. My band was suited, tied, and ready to go with pointy shoes, and then that comes along and you don't want the suit and the shoes anymore. You want to be ragged.

Back in '62 we didn't know what we should be doing. There was a whole rumble of this stuff coming over. It was so crude and lovable and accessible. There was no way you could not like it if you were a dirty boy. I opted for that because I didn't want to be on TV and polished and put in a slot. It was rebellious; the Rolling Stones jumped on that bandwagon. In the early days that's all they did was play Muddy Waters songs, with the freedom to do what they wanted. You didn't have to play the solo exactly the same—you could do what the hell you wanted. But I bet you the Stones got more of their fair share of people coming up and saying, "Can you play something good, something pop?" 'Cause people couldn't dance to it. It kept stopping all the time. Most English kids haven't got the rhythm they were born with. They clap on the downbeat instead of the backbeat. That spells out trouble to me. They haven't got any soul.

**"Smokestack Lightnin' "**
Howlin' Wolf
*Moanin' in the Moonlight*
**JEFF:** That was the first thing I had to learn with the Yardbirds. That was one of their showstoppers. They used to do this buildup and crescendo thing in all their songs, but that was the big one. Driving bass. That was the blueprint for a lot of heavy metal stuff.
**JOHN:** You are a blues guitar player playing with a different background.
**JEFF:** I never lose track of that because it is the most expressive form I know on the guitar.

**"Blue Jean Blues"**
The Jeff Healey Band
*See the Light*
**JEFF:** Stevie Ray Vaughan? Slippery. It sounds like Eric on a good night. It was good. It's got some spirit in it. It's in good form there. I have great fun with this but I usually last for one pass. Though I always love that stuff, I couldn't mold a whole tour around the blues. It's always been a perfect form for some guitar players. It's such a strong chord sequence that nothing has ever come to top it. You could play one note over that whole thing and it would be effective if you played it right. You never grow out of it. You just have to set it aside and spend time trying to develop other things. To do it many times in a night would be too bloody much for me. You'd be saying the same thing over and over again. You'd do a slightly more burning solo or slightly rearrange the phrases, but in essence you're saying the same thing.

# JASON BECKER
# (CACOPHONY, DAVID LEE ROTH)

**"Highway 61 Revisited"**
Johnny Winter
*Second Winter*
**JASON:** Ripping! I've never heard this before. He's got a good song to work with and he does it great. Every lick in there was interesting. Great phrasing. Oh man, he is smoking. I'm gonna buy more Johnny Winter, 'cause I've always been turned off by the slide thing, but it's a good thing when it's done right. Man, he did this song really good all the way through. It's constantly interesting. Every lick blows you away. He stuck with the song and only put good guitar on. This guitar should have been on the original. He plays like a man, which is a good thing.

I hear a lot of players that play and don't really feel it. They don't dig in. They don't have vibrato. Hendrix always played like a man. There's nothing wrong with playing like a woman but there's something about aggression. George Lynch plays like a man. He hits the strings with conviction and it still has soul. He still has feeling in there. It's raw, it's part of the rock 'n' roll energy. It's just a matter of digging into the string. On this tune Johnny Winter was incredible. Every lick was interesting. I wish I could go into it more, but when I like a tune, I just like it.
**JOHN:** Blues was not something you started off exploring.

**JASON:** The blues I was playing was pentatonic, but it wasn't the "blues feel." It was my own feel playing blues. There's nothing wrong with that, but I wanted it to be more authentic. I wanted a few songs to really be blues because old blues men would come up to me and say, "I bet you can't play the blues." I'd play my version of the blues and they'd say, "Nope, I didn't think so." That happened one too many times, so I decided to go find out what they were talking about. I don't think you have to be sad to play blues. I was 11 or 12 when I saw *The Last Waltz.* That's when I got into Clapton. I said, Wow, what's that?

**"Hideaway"**
John Mayall & the Bluesbreakers
*Blues Breakers with Eric Clapton*
**JASON:** This guy sounds more like an old player. He's probably a groundbreaker and I'm being real young, which I am. It doesn't do anything for me. It's just blues licks that are played fairly decently. It's funny when people say they've learned on the streets. People think that's more impressive than playing something else. This guy is great for what he's doing, but I don't like this kind of thing. I like Roy Buchanan, I like Jeff Healey and Stevie Ray Vaughan.
**JOHN:** That was Eric Clapton with John Mayall's Bluesbreakers.
**JASON:** You're kidding. Eric Clapton was my first lead guitar influence. I started listening from his solo stuff. I heard the Cream stuff and all that, but for me he got great when he started his solo stuff. My favorite thing he's ever done is "Further On Up the Road," with the Band. *The Last Waltz* album, with Robbie Robertson and Eric, is why I play lead guitar. I'm embarrassed, but I didn't like this cut.

# NUNO BETTENCOURT (EXTREME)

**"Yer Blues"**
The Dirty Mac
*The Rolling Stones Rock and Roll Circus*
**NUNO:** I think it's always interesting hearing John Lennon doing a blues song. A lot of the mainstream Beatles fans, as I was, don't hear a lot of that. It's great. It seems like he's locked into the track. I was actually surprised. That was Keith Richards?
**JOHN:** He was playing bass. Clapton was fresh off of Cream, Mitch Mitchell was with Jimi.
**NUNO:** Wow, what a line up. It's great. You can hear so much liberation in the vocal. You can hear the fun of it. The fun of it I think is an important factor. You can tell when somebody is having a blast and when they are just punching in the clock.

**"How Come U Don't Call Me Anymore?"**
Prince
*The Hits/The B-Sides*
**NUNO:** This is a good example, in a very different way, of what I'm about. Stylistically telling the world to go fuck themselves, I'll do what I want. He has always been an inspiration in that way. I haven't heard this. It's a great performance. He has great rhythm. That is important.

My suggestion to anyone looking for advice about playing guitar or any other instrument is to play drums first. Learn about it for six months or a year and understand it because it will help your pocket and you're playing incredibly. A lot of the people that I like as rhythm players, whether it be Eddie Van Halen or Prince, all played drums at some point in their life. Al Di Meola is still playing drums on his guitar.

This Prince song is a good example of when somebody does something on their own, how confident they are in their own element. That's always the sign of a great artist, when they really change a lot throughout a record. That's when you know somebody is putting a lot of themselves into it. It's like [Jimmy] Page. You hear him and he would be slobbering through a track almost like it was his first day on the job. Then there's days he would pull off stuff that was so amazing. I think that has a lot to do with somebody putting themselves into the track at that moment. Not every day you feel like you've got it. I think that's the beauty and I think that's something that I am realizing as I go on, to not worry so much. That you have to convince everybody that you have it all the time, or that you clean it up or fix it all the time. Allow yourself to open up. It is being naked and saying, Hey I know this solo isn't the best in the world but that's what I felt at the time I did the track, so here it is. Instead of saying, My god it's for life and it's going to change the world.

There was a time when every time I did a solo, I had to cure cancer. It was, My god, if somebody is going to hear this, they are going to die if it's not perfect. I'm glad I did that. I still think I did some of the best stuff that way. But I don't blame anybody or anyone or anything that happens to me. I am in complete control of myself. I'm not into saying he did it, he made me do it. I'm too selfish for that. I am too in control of myself. I can say no at any moment. Nobody is forcing me to do anything. If I wanted to make it perfect that day, I did that. If that's where my head space was at. Now, if I want to make it more spontaneous, I do that. That's the most important thing. That's sleeping at night. Doing what you love to do.

# MICHAEL BLOOMFIELD (THE PAUL BUTTERFIELD BLUES BAND, ELECTRIC FLAG)

**"I'm a Fool"**
Larry Carlton
*Mr. 335 Live in Japan*
**MICHAEL:** It's good. It's an unaffected singer. Sounds a little like Dr. John. The instrumentation was sparse, but not too sparse. The guitar sounds like me. It's real good. Who is this?
**JOHN:** Larry Carlton.
**MICHAEL:** That was Larry? Doesn't sound like Larry's playing. If you listen to a lot of his playing, he uses the volume pedal a lot. Sometimes I find his most interesting playing is on a TV soundtrack.

**"De Rabbit"**
Eric Gale
*Ginseng Woman*
**MICHAEL:** I don't know who it is and it don't show me anything. Is it Eric Gale? It sounds like Eric's playing; sterile. He's better off with Stuff. He needs Cornell Dupree to keep his ass on the line. That's Eric's dumb, stiff playing. Let me clear this up. When it comes to background or soul guitar, no one can beat Eric. He is not a good lead player. He is not a good bluesman. But for some reason with Cornell and Stuff, it brings out the best in him. This ain't it.

**“Sweet Little Lisa”**
Dave Edmunds (Albert Lee on lead)
*Repeat When Necessary*
**MICHAEL:** Dynamite! Great rockabilly music and great singing. The guitar sounds sort of like Jerry Reed or a little Roy Buchanan. It’s just fine. I have no idea who it is, but that could be a hit.

**‘Straight from the Heart”**
Little Feat
*Down on the Farm*
**MICHAEL:** The guitar playing sounds like some sort of Ry Cooder imitation. It’s not quite as good as Ry. It’s a good funk arrangement but it doesn’t show me a whole lot. I’m real curious about who it is.
**JOHN:** That was Lowell George
**MICHAEL:** I thought it was Lowell. I’ve heard him sing and play a lot more expressively than that. I don’t want to say this about no dead person, so let’s just cut it right here.

**“The Final Peace”**
Jeff Beck
*There & Back*
**MICHAEL:** I loved the use of the string machine, or whatever it was. I think the guitar player was too dramatic. The phrasing was emotional but to me it was schmaltzy. He was trying too hard. I like the pathos he was trying to get out of his playing. But in conjunction with that background, he could have done more. He used five notes. He used the blues scale with a nice touch. Who was that?
**JOHN:** Jeff Beck
**MICHAEL:** I’m used to hearing Jeff play something off the wall. He didn’t do that this time. He just played the notes. I’m used to Jeff taking chances. He didn’t on this one. He wasn’t taking any

risks at all, and that's why I didn't like it so much.
**JOHN:** Jeff Beck is among the most vocalistic of electric guitar players. That's some of what makes him a stylist.
**MICHAEL:** Blues is basically a vocal music, not an instrumental music. And the best blues players play their instruments real vocally. So it sounds like a human voice. That's why you use slides and things that can emulate the facility, the slide the human voice has. Because the voice can slide up anywhere it wants to.

When this music style first started in this country, 200 years ago, a little more than that, there was very little to work with as far as the scale. There was one scale five notes long. Each note could be changed and altered, and the register lowered. But black people in this country at that time who brought their music with them ran into American music, which was really English music, hymns and Protestant music. It had not the blues scale, but the regular major scale.

When the two musical cultures met, they took this scale and adapted it to an old vocal tradition, which is not hitting the notes right on but playing with them a little. All music is tinted with the blues notes in this way. The highest bluesy music is gospel music, as opposed to blues. The style of singing or playing uses a lot of bent notes, especially vocal.

That style, there is an Italian word for it, it's called *melisma.* What melisma means is if you're singing a word and the word has one syllable and you give it more than one syllable, each syllable being a note, that is called melismatic singing. You can use this as your vehicle for blues notes in vocal performances. I'll give you an example. If you sing the word *you* and you're singing the blues and use more than one syllable, each one being a note you go [sings and plays]. This is melismatic singing, using one syllable as a vehicle for singing blues notes. If you listen to a singer like Aretha, who is a highly melismatic singer, or Sly or Rufus, they use tremendous amounts of notes in just singing one word. They use a few words for a huge amount of vocal improvisation.

# VITO BRATTA (WHITE LION)

**"Say What!"**
Stevie Ray Vaughan
*Live at Montreux 1985*
**VITO**: For a while I was listening to Gary Moore a lot and then Stevie came out. In the summer of '88 I made a compilation of his first three records on a 90-minute cassette. I couldn't get that one cassette out of my head. I love everything about this guy. It's the whole attitude and sound and feel that he has. Plus, you really couldn't get too many blues records with that kind of playing. You could listen to Hendrix. I was dying to get Stevie's live version of "Voodoo Chile" when it first came out. When I finally got it, I was disappointed. There wasn't a lot of energy coming from this recording. He really wasn't going for it. But then I said to myself, I guess that just goes to show that he goes for it in the studio. I was expecting a lot more.

# J. J. CALE

**"Calling Elvis"**
Dire Straits
*On Every Street*

**J. J.:** I know this song. That's kind of his style of singing. "Calling Elvis" wasn't a huge hit for Dire Straits but it got played on the radio a lot.

**JOHN:** Mark Knopfler is very eloquent with his silence and so are you.

**J. J.:** On some days.

**JOHN:** Did you ever overplay?

**J. J.:** Oh yes, still do. If you'd seen when I played Atlanta, Georgia, a few nights ago and had a pretty good size band, three guitars, two synthesizers, two drums, bass player. Before the evening was through I was definitely overplaying. I started off overplaying. The reason I got into playing not so many [notes] was because everybody else sounded like they were overplaying and I wanted to try and stand out from everything else that was going on in the late '60s and '70s. So I kind of slowed everything down and made everything a little sparser. At that time everything was pretty much in-your-face kind of music. I kind of made it sound different from everybody else. That's the whole trick.

**JOHN:** And that changed your guitar playing?

**J. J.:** I decided I was no longer just a guitar player anymore. I was becoming successful as a songwriter. So, I started making everything more sparse so I could get the song across. If you play a lot, sometimes the song gets lost. I was trying to sell songs. It was much more profitable a business then, playing the guitar. I think the reason I did that was, I was starting to become more of a songwriter and less of a guitar player in a band.

**"Black Friday"**
Steely Dan
*Katy Lied*
**J. J.:** They tried to make it a little more complex. That's Steely Dan. It's a vocal that I identify. It's a song people can relate to and adds sophistication. Also, it's fun to make chordings, doing multiple stuff. Sometimes I put more stuff on it and after I listen I think I should have left about half of it off. But that's fun doing that. It's a process. Playing your guitar into tape recorders in studios and all that stuff you can do nowadays, is kind of an art form in itself. It's like painting a picture. Once you get done, you're done with it. It's kind of a trip, with all the modern tracking. The new technology with all the tracks and stuff, you can put yourself on 100 times. Sometimes I'm sure I'm not the only one, but you go past. You put out records and think, Well, I put too much stuff on that. I wish I had stopped.

**"Reverence"**
Milt Jackson
*Reverence and Compassion*
**J. J.:** Is the vibe player the front guy?
**JOHN:** It's Milt Jackson.
**J. J.:** That was an era when this was more popular than, say, it is now.
**JOHN:** I notice that you like the vibes and have a touch of jazz in some of your songs.
**J. J.:** The vibes on my latest record is a synthesizer. What I heard was more cocktail jazz, which you don't really hear that much.

Most of the modern jazz is a little more complicated than that. When you say that I do a little bit of jazz, I write in that vein. Some of my songs I used to play at those kinds of gigs. Playing those gigs back in the early part of my life, when I was playing guitar, I played that style, every once in a while. When I got into writing songs for a living, I would always go back and go, Yeah, I like that. It was kind of jive jazz. This is cocktail jazz. I write some of my songs in that vein. I like to sing in that vein. Mose Allison is really good as a singer in that vein.

**JOHN:** When you play a synthesized guitar with that vibes sound, are you thinking like a guitarist or a vibes player?

**J. J.:** I'm trying to think like a vibes player, but I don't. What I'm doing is remembering what I've heard good vibes player do and then imitating them, which is never as good as they could do it. I'm using it as an effect to create a mood and hoping people don't bust me that it's not really a good vibes player. I like the mood it sets that song into, the flavor. It's like sauce on different kinds of food. You can take this regular hamburger and you can start putting stuff on it and pretty soon it changes.

**JOHN:** What is attractive about the vibes as an instrument?

**J. J.:** It has a mellow tone. Kind of like a trombone. It's in those frequencies. Maybe it's the vibrato. It's a flavor and it makes the recording have a certain flavor.

# LARRY CARLTON

**"Say it (Over and Over Again)"**
John Coltrane
*Ballads*
**LARRY:** John Coltrane playing a beautiful melody. I don't remember the name of it because it's not important. It's understated. He is playing with warmth and feel and tone and picked a song that has a wonderful melody. There is nothing to impress you with technique, still it takes tons of technique to be able to play those opening notes and have it immediately grab me. A great lesson, as I've said, in the past for anyone who wonders how to play a song. Try to play the melody and make it feel and sound like something. Forget about soloing. Forget about technique or the blues. Take a song, a well-written tune and make a room calm down in two bars. That's what John did. The opening notes and the whole mood of everything is commanded by that man's horn. It takes hard work, diligence and the big gift.
**JOHN:** Is that how you approach a melody?
**LARRY:** Definitely. There are notes on the guitar that I pick very hard with the right hand, but I get so little piece of the note that it sounds very delicate. It's backwards. There's a lot of effort to sound gentle. John is the man for me. He knows how to play a melody.
**JOHN:** Where are you the proudest of yourself for playing the melody?

**LARRY:** A good example would be "Emotions Wound Us So" from *Last Nite*.
**JOHN:** Rik Emmet [Triumph] picked that song as solo of the year.

**"Don't Want You No More" / "It's Not My Cross to Bear"**
Gregg Allman
*I'm No Angel*
**LARRY:** I enjoyed the tone on the guitar, the sound. The overall performance of the whole thing sounded like somebody took all the heart out of it so it would go on tape clean. That's the way my ears perceived it. It was the blues being played much too cleanly. Even the recording quality was real hi-fi. I didn't get the emotion of five guys into that tune. I got separation of sound. It sounded safe. I felt real safe. No surprises, only in the arrangement. Then it was played to a tee. The arrangement was nice and it's like, Yes, we did it, not, Yeah, we got it. It was, Yes, we did it.
**JOHN:** Is that the way it was recorded or played?
**LARRY:** Both. It could be recorded as cleanly as it was, but I felt that those guys made it sound like it was from the studio rather than from their hearts. This is the way I will play in the studio. I will play precisely. If my perception is right, they either haven't spent much time in the studio, so they are free no matter the circumstance, or that's the way they play. I don't know that. It was a little cautious for me on all parts. He definitely has a feel for the blues, he just sounded so safe, so rehearsed. This is what I want them to hear me do this time rather than this is what I do, and I'd like them to hear that. It felt a little squeaky clean.

This gentleman who played on the Gregg Allman track, I heard direct cops of my licks. I heard one in there note for note. I watched it go by. It hadn't become his yet. It was just a set of notes. There is a way and a time that lick will become his. It won't sound like a Larry Carlton lick and I probably learned it from Robben [Ford]. We all do it. To make them our own is where personality comes in.

# PHIL COLLEN (DEF LEPPARD)

**"My Head's in Mississippi"**
ZZ Top
*Recycler*
**PHIL:** That's Billy Gibbons with "Head's in Miss." I love ZZ Top, always have. I was in a band years ago that used to do ZZ Top song covers in London, when no one had even heard of them. I did "La Grange," "Tush," "Thunderbird." That's how I first learned harmonics, by listening to Billy Gibbons. "La Grange" has harmonics all over the place and I actually learned off of that record how to do them. I've got a real soft spot for him.

This song reminds me of a '90s version of "La Grange." The first time I heard it I thought, Wow that's obviously what they tried to do and they pulled it off. They are unique and they stay fresh. Billy Gibbons has his finger on the pulse. They use drum machines and sequencer which keeps them up to date. His lyrics are really hip and he has such a soulful voice. With ZZ Top it's done with such a sense of humor and tongue in cheek. It's like David Lee Roth could pull things off because he's that type of character. It's the same kind of thing.

# ROBERT CRAY

**"Something"**
The Beatles
*Abbey Road*
**ROBERT:** Listen to George Harrison. I like that song. I never figured out how he does that, if he's playing slide or what on that. That's a great sound, though, and it sounds like that Leslie guitar. It sounds really cool. I wouldn't change a thing on that song. It's just a nice, simple tune and it's got that melody line [sings line]. It's just cool 'cause it's really smooth and it's also cool 'cause it's George Harrison and I like George Harrison and how he sounds. It's like when I was young enough and started to play guitar, I wanted to play guitar 'cause the Beatles were out [laughs]. So I have a weak spot for George Harrison.

I was just enthused about the whole thing with the British invasion coming to America and everybody in my neighborhood got a guitar when all that stuff started happening. It became the most popular instrument and the Beatles were playing and shaking their hair and everything like that. When we were coming up, we tried to play just about everything on the radio, like "Taxman" and "Day Tripper." I was taking guitar lessons at the time too, so "Day Tripper" was one that I was down with.

**“Can I Change My Mind”**
Tyrone Davis
*Greatest Hits*
**ROBERT:** If I remember right, I think Phil Upchurch is playing. Is Phil Upchurch playing bass on this stuff? Either that or he’s playing guitar. It cracks me up because the guitar line is a little bit much. It’s too busy, but it’s a Tyrone Davis song so everything’s cool, you know. I dig Tyrone Davis. He’s Mr. Smooth, Mr. Mellow. Well, I like this kind of style.

You remember in the ’60s and maybe into the ’70s a little bit, some of those songs used to have the vibe sound, a pretty bell sound on some of them. I don’t know where that type of music was from; I want to say it was probably something East Coast like, but I can’t really put my finger on where the music was coming from. But it was pretty cool, that soul kind of thing. And we have a weakness for that kind of music, Jim [Pugh, keyboards] and I do. And you know what happens when you get caught listening to something at the same time you’re writing—it’s gonna pop up in there, and that’s what happens.
**JOHN:** You’re saying you still listen to the same records?
**ROBERT:** Yeah, I’m still listening. You know, it depends on what day it is. I’ll be listening to Tyrone. I got the greatest hits of Tyrone Davis on CD [laughs]. There’s a nice ballad I like on there, “I Wish It Was Me,” which is a great tune. I have a weakness for a ballad. I love slow ballads, soulful ballads, and the slower and the more passionate they are, the more I’m a fool for them. I mean, we have to have a ballad; I mean, that’s a definite. We’re going to have a ballad on every album.

**“Green Onions”**
Booker T. & the MG’s
*The Best of Booker T. & the MG’s*
**ROBERT:** That’s a funky sound on the guitar. That’s an extremely funky tune, always has been and always will be. It’s funny be-

cause we were with Steve [Cropper] in Seville in Spain and we sat down, and he was writing me his address. He wrote left-handed. I said, “Steve, you’re left-handed.” He says, “Yeah.” I say, “How come you play guitar right-handed? Why didn’t you just get a left-handed guitar?” He said, “All the guitars in the shop came right-handed. So that’s how I play. That’s how Duck Dunn plays too.”

I noticed his hands when he plays, and it looks a little like he’s uncomfortable. Maybe being left-handed there is a different kind of approach you have when your hand is not the one that is supposed to be on the fingerboard. It’s weird. Steve has a great sound. I like his sound. “Green Onions” is a funky tune. It’s just those parts that make the whole thing sound good. It’s as simple as it wants to be but it’s a very dynamic song.

**“Don’t Know Which Way to Go”**
Buddy Guy
*Rush: Music from the Motion Picture Soundtrack*
**ROBERT:** It’s got that Buddy Guy sound but I’m not sure if it’s Buddy or not yet. I couldn’t tell if it was Buddy or not because he hadn’t gone crazy earlier. I was thinking Buddy would play more at the intro of this song. There’s a couple other guitar players playing rhythm behind him. Is this a Royal Albert Hall thing? It’s Buddy Guy.
**JOHN:** Could you tell from the rhythm playing?
**ROBERT:** Yeah, he played a fill back there too. But then I just wanted to make sure before I said anything. Buddy’s already a maniacal guitar player and he’s puttin’ an Echoplex on it; it just excites me more. This is really good Buddy Guy; I like it. Buddy plays a Strat like it has that real Stratocaster sound. And you could tell it was kind of Buddy, but I wasn’t sure because it was taking a bit too much time for the Buddy Guy style that I normally associate with being Buddy Guy’s guitar style.
**JOHN:** Which is more aggressive?

**ROBERT:** More aggressive; then you could tell, and as soon as he opened up his mouth, I mean, yeah, Buddy Guy, his high, great voice. It was pretty cool; I dug that. There was one turnaround he stuck in a fill, and it was like, fleet fingered, you know? He makes the guitar sing, the way when he hits those high notes [imitates notes].

**"Cold Day in Hell"**
Gary Moore
*After Hours*
**ROBERT:** It's kind of too strong for me. It's not in my taste. It's a little bit overdone. The guitarist didn't work too much. The sustain is not the normal sustain you'd find running straight through an amplifier. That kind of bugs me. I didn't care too much for the singing either. I don't know if I can make it through the rest of the tune [laughs]. I wouldn't listen to it. It wouldn't be in my record stack.
**JOHN:** It's Gary Moore.
**ROBERT:** I kind of thought so. I've heard him do "Still Got the Blues," which is a more subdued song. I like listening to that. I've heard that on the radio over in Europe. I've also seen him do a thing with Albert Collins where they have a video together. They're doing "Too Tired." It was great to see Albert Collins on TV. That put a big smile on my face. But sorry, Gary, I don't like this one. It's just a bit too much for me. I think it's a little bit over the top. He pushed too hard. He's a great guitar player but I don't think he gets the point across to me in this particular number. The background singing is not what I like. I don't like it when he hits the high octaves. It's too strong; there's too much stuff on the guitar.

**“Soldier of Fortune”**
Sonny Landreth
*Outward Bound*
**ROBERT:** There was good playing going on and that was a good song till they hyped it up. I could listen to the whole song till the fuzz tones came in. That’s good playing. I don’t know who that was.
**JOHN:** Sonny Landreth.
**ROBERT:** I know Sonny. That was good. Sonny is a great player. He is all around. First of all it’s a good song. I like the way he opened up the tune. He was playing some kind of open thing maybe on the top of the neck. It sounded really good. Really smooth playing. I like the way the guitars meshed. He’s a great country style player. Good picking.
**JOHN:** You didn’t like it when the band came in.
**ROBERT:** No, I like that whole feel before. I thought it was going to come back around the verse again. I’m not one of those heavy monster guys. Just give me a song nice and simple. I didn’t like that. Sorry, Sonny; I like you though, man. I hate to make my opinions known about other players. Sonny is a bastard man. He was so gorgeous when he played with Hyatt. “Lipstick Sunset” is a great song. This was a good solo. I have to say the uptempo part just hit me too hard. I liked it when he went back. The first part of the solo, I like the guitar tone. I was caught by surprise by the second part. I didn’t know if it was another player or a different instrument that he was playing. I prefer the sound of the first part. It was a whole different style. My ears are tuned to maybe a certain frequency that appeals to me. After a while it gets kind of difficult for me to listen to.

**"Ladies' Nite In Buffalo?"**
David Lee Roth
*Eat 'Em and Smile*
**ROBERT:** Is that Van Halen or somebody? I don't know who it is. I liked it because it was a funky rock tune. The front part of it I could hear the Hendrix influence. That was pretty cool. I was basically trying to listen to the guitar. The song was good, I guess. I was captivated by the Hendrix influence. I'm a Hendrix fan too. The comping he was doing in the beginning the intro, the octaves. That hit me with the Hendrix thing.
**JOHN:** That was David Lee Roth with Steve Vai.
**ROBERT:** I can't see how people play so fast though. It was a very interesting solo. There was some cool way he got around to making the changes in the first part of that solo. But it was quicker than shit. I listen in amazement. It was great. I don't listen to this kind of style, so I'm listening with new ears; impressive. That's a whole different world from what I know.

**"Friends"**
Joe Satriani
*The Extremist*
**ROBERT:** It amazes me that somebody moves around that fast with that control and that sound. You take that song and you could slow it down a little bit and maybe play it on acoustic guitar. It might sound pretty good. The way it is right now I guess what they are looking for is that heavy thing. For some reason it struck me that it might sound really good played on a couple of acoustic guitars. It doesn't strike a nerve on me. It's not anything that would consume my interest for any amount of time. The cat can play. It struck me that I could hear that quieter.

**"T-Bone Shuffle"**
Albert Collins/Robert Cray/Johnny Copeland
*Showdown!*

**ROBERT:** "T-Bone Shuffle" with Albert Collins. Did Johnny Copeland play on that one too? That was fun making that record. I don't know that we should have done that song, when I think about it now. We used to do this song with our own band. I think it was put on the record for lack of anything else to do. I was so used to hearing my band doing it our way as opposed to having a band that hasn't played it that much the way I'm used to it. So when I hear it I go, That's not the way it's supposed to go.

**JOHN:** This was one of the great sittin' in records.

**ROBERT:** That was fun. We've done a lot of work with Albert before. It was fun to do. It came together so quick. There was hardly any time spent in production for the record. It was just a matter of getting together and doing it. Bruce Iglauer likes to do that with his records. We spent a short time on this. Bruce Bromberg and I had time to pen one song.

**JOHN:** Did it deserve the Grammy it won?

**ROBERT:** I don't know. It was just a fun thing to do. We did it so quickly.

## CHRIS DEGARMO, MICHAEL WILTON (QUEENSRŸCHE)

**"The Telephone Song"**
The Vaughan Brothers
*Family Style*

**CHRIS:** I don't know. It's cool jamming. I can appreciate it but it's not the kind of stuff I'd sit around and listen to.

**MICHAEL:** It sounds like it would be really fun to play. The wah-wah and all that, sounds a bit Hendrixy. The blues scale. It's good. The playing is very solid.

**CHRIS:** I particularly like the rhythm guitar arrangement on that. It's got a good funk sort of pick to it. It's obviously good performances but stylistically it's not my cup of tea. It sounded to me like it was Stevie Ray Vaughan.

**MICHAEL:** Yeah.

**CHRIS:** We both knew it was Stevie Ray Vaughan. We do a lot of listening to a lot of music, so we're aware of it and can appreciate where other people are coming from. One thing that we'll never say is that our way is the only way. Fortunately, there's enough room in this business for everyone to do what their passion is. Stevie's whole reputation was as a smokin' blues guitar player. He comes from a family of smokin' blues guitar players, and they have a passion about what they do, and a lot of people relate to it, and we can appreciate that, but it's not the kind of style that both of us choose to write. It's not that we can't appreciate it from a listening standpoint. It's just when it comes to writing stuff we go for something different. I think, for instance, when we go in to record we'll bring the stuff about 70 percent to completion, and we leave a certain percentage of the stuff open for whatever inspiration happens, once we're actually into the studio.

**MICHAEL:** Those are things that you usually remember the most, the kind of things that just spark, like a strange feedback, or you get something that's hard to duplicate.

**CHRIS:** Though there is spontaneity in Queensrÿche music, it's generally at the compositional end, and when it's on the performance end it just happens to be tight as well.

**JOHN:** For all of your modern progressive vision on the guitar, I believe you started off with the blues.

**MICHAEL:** When I got off the road recently, I went back to my blues roots. I kind of went full circle. I searched for what got me started playing guitar in the first place. By the time the Empire tour ended, I just pulled out old blues records. I went out and bought an Elmore James boxed set. I'm a big fan of Duane Allman and I just listened to Elmore James over and over again. I hear the Allman Brothers and knew this is what he listened too.

It's so amazing. Those old blues players were really just heart and soul. They really got into it. That's what I kind of got into. I started retracing that. I had to go back and see what made this fun for me in the beginning. That's where I've been. You've heard this a million times, but I was playing the blues. Jamming with the blues, that's just pure expression, pure freedom. You close your eyes and you don't care about anything. You just play whatever you want. That brought me back.

## WARREN DEMARTINI (RATT)

**"In Time"**
Maceo Parker
*Roots Revisited*
**WARREN:** Maceo is one of my favorite players and a monumental influence. This comes from one of my favorite albums, *Roots Revisited.* It's unabridged Maceo probably playing his favorite songs. Although I like him on James Brown's music too, a lot of times with James the solo stuff isn't that long. Here you can hear him get into some good improvisation. It's one of the few times that somebody has pulled off covering a song doing it in their own feel and having it stand up to the original. The feel from Sly Stone's original isn't derailed in the translation.

What interests me about horns is that with the guitar you learn your patterns and your scales from the shapes on the instrument. With horns, piano, and the more chromatic instruments you probably learn things in modes as opposed to shapes. That's why I like listening to and learning from horns. It doesn't sound like there are any barriers when you run into a good horn player, especially with major keys. It just sounds very natural. I think it's a different part of your brain. On the guitar there are modes that you play in that are just kind of standard modes for guitar. With a horn it seems much more personal to the actual music. You know, the grass is always greener. It awakens the part of the mind that listens to what is not being played as well as what is being played.

Something about Maceo's playing really nails it for me. The way he plays in the holes and in the pockets, and the sound that he creates in the places that he doesn't play, make his playing that much more punchy. It's a combination of his choice of notes plus the sound he gets out of that horn.

To me the sax is the perfect lead instrument because it creates its own distortion. It's a natural distortion and a real pleasant one to my ear. It's also kind of voltage controlled where the harder he hits it the more it breaks up, like an old Marshall. To me, the great thing about old Marshalls is the harder you hit the string the more they break up and vice versa, which is unique in an amp. Because most amps have a very linear thing where no matter how you play it, it kind of comes out the same. To me a very good amp is the soft to loud as well as the overall tone, which kind of took me a while to get hip to.

**"Little Red Rooster"**
The Rolling Stones (with Eric Clapton)
*Flashpoint*
**WARREN:** Clapton with the Stones. He was on fire that night. I remember, I saw that show. It was like a rebirth of Clapton the way he was playing in the late '60s. There was just something about it. He was really on that night. He kind of gave up the "Slowhand" thing for a night and burned. I thought he really played good on that. It seemed like he was really wound up.

And what can you say about the Stones? I was listening to *Sticky Fingers* the other day. On the credits it said thanks to this engineer and that engineer and everybody else who sat through the two millions hours it took to do this. It occurred to me they probably took a year or two and did it piece by piece and really came up with a unique feel and unique songs and vibes. Judging from that statement, they probably pieced it together a little bit at a time. Mick Taylor was there. That was probably my favorite lineup. Mick Taylor added a kind of musicianship that I don't think they have regained.

**"Night and Day"**
Joe Pass
*Guitar Player Presents Legends of Guitar: Jazz, Vol. 2*
**WARREN:** Is this Joe Pass? Wow! It's awesome to listen to somebody improvise like that. I haven't heard too many people that can do that. Playing rock, you improvise, but not to the extent that someone like Joe Pass does. That sounds like 100 percent off the cuff.

I loved that he was able to spill over the line between even and odd, to keep a meter going in your head and play on the upbeat for a while and then play through the bars. Being able to do that is something I've mentally been working on for a few years. It's a neat thing listening to someone play like that, with nothing else audibly keeping the time. Having somebody go in and out of bars like that and also kind of spilling over in an odd way and then coming back out to it, it's kind of like what Jon Bonham would do.
**JOHN:** Is rock improvisation a poor stepchild to jazz improvs?
**WARREN:** It's a different animal. When you start getting into structured songs, the art of improvising is lost. That song is probably something he has worked on a lot, but it sounds like he is just thinking it up as he goes along. There is a certain transparency with jazz songs. It's just a style, a mood. People can do jazz standards their own way and it sounds new, it sounds them.

Can you imagine this thing with Bach and Beethoven, and those kinds of composers? From what I've heard, their ability to improvise was unbelievable. They could just sit down and play something perfectly that they had never played before. And they make it up as they were going along! Some of the stuff was obviously written out and worked on. But they were also able to improvise. It's something I keep in mind, to kind of work out songs but also to be striving to be able to do that because it can be done. But it's being familiar with the fretboard well enough to let your mind wander and be able to play whatever you think. I think that is the final level you get too.

# AL DI MEOLA

**"Goodbye Pork Pie Hat"**
Jeff Beck
*Wired*

**AL:** That's Jeff Beck, "Goodbye Pork Pie Hat." It's probably the best piece on the album. His phrasing, his sound is fantastic. I haven't heard that in a while and playing that for me now is really nice and refreshing. I'd give that a five. It's my favorite blues piece. I'm not a blues fanatic at all, but I like that very much. It's very well played, especially his phrasing, and he displays it well on this piece. It's nice to listen to a piece that slow moving and mellow, especially with a Strat. You can do that with a Strat. I love Jeff Beck, especially when he does tunes like this. He's trying other things now; he's not sticking to the rock and roll bag, which can be real limiting. He's getting out there, he's expanding.

## RIK EMMETT (TRIUMPH)

**"Can't Get Enough"**
Bad Company
*Bad Company*
**RIK:** That's classic blues riffing. Mick's real good at that kind of thing, great feel, great groove. It's a classic simple chord guitar hit, along with things like "Whole Lotta Love." It's classic because it's a tune that a great player can play and sound good and a kid in his basement can play and sound good. It's a simple song that relies more on feel than anything else. A kid could get into it and play it and sound good or a sophisticated player can play the same thing and be faced with the same challenge.

Jimmy Page was turned on to the guitar by the blues guys. They didn't care if it was in tune or not; they just did it. There was a real atmosphere about that.

Anything is hard to write. There's a misconception that people think to write something in 7/4 with six bars of 5/4 and modulate up a minor third is hard. Then they think it's easy to do the other thing, but it's not. They are all hard. Nothing comes easy. The hard thing is to write a song like this and make it feel good and flow.

**"Sultans of Swing"**
Dire Straits
*Dire Strait*
**RIK:** I love this because I love blues playing. I love blues in rock. This guy I love because of his phrasing and the sort of hybrid thing. He is playing a rock tune but it's more like a swing kind of thing and he's playing with his fingers and he's chicken plucking and it's almost as if he were playing an acoustic or playing on a nylon string but he's playing on an electric. He gets great tones. He's a really warm emotional kind of player and he's almost the complete package.

The only thing that Mark Knopfler lacks a bit is he hasn't got a real warm easy kind of voice. You've got to develop a taste for it, like Bob Dylan's. His playing and his songwriting are really good. This song is where it all started for him in terms of getting what he does across to the general public. He had a sound, he had a style, and he had a songwriting thing. I own tons of his stuff, even the film scores. *Local Hero* is my wife's favorite music to play around the house.

# BUZZ FEITEN, NEIL LARSEN (FULL MOON, LARSEN-FEITEN BAND)

**"I Can See Clearly Now"**
Ray Charles
*True to Life*

**NEIL:** That's Ray. I like everything he does, but I like his older stuff. I'm really into Ray Charles from the early '60s. I just got a record before I left and I listened to that a lot. There's one tune, I think it's "Blackjack," where he plays the whole tune with a trio and the last two chords are like a 20-piece band going "dan done!" That's the ear of Ray Charles that really kills me. But I say everything he does is great.

**BUZZ:** One of my favorite things that he did recently is the tune called "The Jealous Kind" *[True to Life]*. I'm real partial to organs playing the backbeat. "Looking for Clues" by Robert Palmer has got that too. I get that from listening to the Rascals. That's all they did. "The Jealous Kind" is my favorite tune that he's done recently."

**"My Funny Valentine"**
Bill Evans and Jim Hall
*Undercurrent*

**NEIL:** *Undercurrent,* right? I like Bill Evans most on ballads where he tears your heart out, like on *Kind of Blue*. He wrote the notes on *Kind of Blue*.

**BUZZ:** I'm always jealous of guys that play like that because I can't. It's great to hear somebody that can do all that shit with passing chords.
**NEIL:** Actually, I like playing that kind of thing more than listening to it. Buzz and I play together and get into things like that, that sort of direction.
**BUZZ:** It's like an art form that's very rigid. It's got very specific rules of things you can and can't do. Listening to it is almost like listening to a dead art form. It's great and it's to be admired. But it doesn't stimulate me at all. It's become so standard. These guys were the pioneers; they invented it.
**NEIL:** I think that's what happens a lot. Someone will come along and invent a whole new style of playing. Jimmy Smith is a great example. He's emulated so much, it takes the edge off the way he originally did it. His sound has become a staple, so that it takes a little heat away from what he was originally doing. This is from an old record and when it came out it was really different.

**"Wait Until Tomorrow"**
Jimi Hendrix Experience
*Axis: Bold As Love*
**BUZZ:** We play that every sound check. That's the lick that I test my guitar sound on. I swear to God. Once I get the sound, that's the lick. What can you say about him? There's nothing to say; it's been said. Wish he were here. He reinvented the Stratocaster. He reinstated that sound. I love everything that comes out of his music. I don't feel that I'm qualified or in a position to say he's this or that. I can't say anything except I love the sound of his guitar. It's so clear. You can hear every note, every string. Then there's the fact that the guy wasn't afraid to play simple. He had the balls to play simple, to play what he felt. That's what comes though. He plays a little solo in this, in the rhythm, and he fits it in.
**JOHN:** Tell me how you got your first professional gig, with Paul Butterfield; from jamming with Hendrix and B.B. King?

**BUZZ:** I was 18 at the time. While I was at Mannes College in New York, I met Elvin Bishop through a friend of a friend. Elvin invited me to jam with the band. After the set there was a jam session which started at one a.m. with B.B. King, Paul Butterfield, Elvin Bishop, Phillip Wilson, Al Kooper and Jimi Hendrix. I sat in on bass until six in the morning. When we left the club, it was light out and Butterfield invited me to come down and audition.

# DON FELDER (EAGLES)

**"Sweet Little Angel"**
B.B. King
*King of the Blues*
**DON:** I grew up listening to that stuff. In Gainesville, all the radio stations were white owned, and they all went off the air at sundown. It was all country music, kind of the white man's version of rock 'n' roll: Pat Boone, and all that stuff. If you really wanted to hear anything great, after all the traffic was off the air, after sundown you could just barely get WLAC in Nashville, Tennessee. They would come in really kind of faint. You'd have to strain to hear that stuff. It was sponsored by Randy's Record Mart and they would play B.B. King, Albert King, whatever that kind of blues flavor was. That was the only way you really got to hear it. Then you could order those records right there on the radio. You'd mail in your $2.95 for that single or whatever it was, from Randy's Record Mart.

WLAC in Nashville had a huge, huge influence on me. You are absolutely right on with that one. That song that we do, "I Can't Tell You Why," was done on a [Gibson ES-] 335 in the studio. But I kind of play this Lucille 355, that black one in the show. It is kind of a salute to B.B., a thank you.

**JOHN:** Did you start because of the likes of a B.B. King?

**DON:** Yeah, that was probably the structure of most of the solos. That kind of minor modal blues influence. It was simple enough.

All the black clubs in the south were illegal. They weren't allowed to have gatherings when I was a kid. There was this kind of illegal bar, literally in this cow pasture, that served keg beer. And me and this friend, when we were just kids, snuck into the back of this club and saw B.B. play. There were women wailing, crying and screaming. They were emotionally moved by his singing and his playing. And listening to him on WLAC had a really strong influence.

**"East St. Louis Toodle-Oo"**
Steely Dan
*Pretzel Logic*
**DON:** Wah wah huh. Who was that?
**JOHN:** Steely Dan.
**DON:** Musically that was pretty flatfooted, less than cool. The techniques were all right but I just thought musically it was flatfooted.
**JOHN:** It was a Duke Ellington tune.
**DON:** Just the way it was done.

## MICHAEL LEE FIRKINS

**"Don't Burn Down the Bridge"**
Otis Rush
*Ain't Enough Comin' In*
**MICHAEL:** Robert Cray? Now I'm not so sure. Is that Jack Bruce singing? Is this Johnny Gale? Is it Eric Clapton singing? It sounds like Robert Cray but the vibrato sounds more modern. Then I was going to say Eric Clapton singing with Robert Cray playing guitar or Jack Bruce singing or something off the Vaughan Brothers album. Is it maybe Jimmy Vaughan playing guitar? He's got more reverb on his sound usually. It sounds for real. This guy sounds for real too but something in his vibrato sounds a little more modern. It was very good authentic blues. If it's not Robert Cray, it sure sounds like him. It sounds a little bit like Stevie Ray Vaughn playing guitar but a lot of people do, so that's kind of hard.
**JOHN:** This is Otis Rush.
**MICHAEL:** I don't know a thing about him. It was good, man, definitely authentic. Good sound too. Memphis horns maybe? It kind of reminded me of Stevie Winwood a little bit. I'm not 100 percent of a blues player, but there is a lot of blues in me. I'm not a 100 percent blues and I don't want to be either. Blues gives everyone a sense of reality of music as you're doing it. Not music as it is tomorrow or as it after you make a record. It's music right then and there. When the song is done, the song is over. It's not stewing about recording, it's now. That's what the blues is to me—it's

now. This is good blues.

**"Day of the Eagle"**
Robin Trower
*Bridge of Sighs*
**MICHAEL:** Killer; that's awesome. This is my favorite kind of blues. My friends played this when I first heard it. This is probably the second time I've ever heard this by him. I've heard other people playing "Day of the Eagle." I want to play this song at one of our gigs. I don't know if he listened to Johnny Winter very much. I opened up for Robin Trower in Tulsa, Oklahoma.

I like this stuff, the minor seventh chord. I like blues songs that don't have to just go I IV V. This is killer droning stuff. Where he goes off into the solo is awesome. I've got to get me some Trower albums. The funk, *chicka chicka* on the rhythms and the Hendrix kind of timing as far as the way the whole band sounds and just everyone comes down for the solo. It kind of drones and he goes off into the solo. I just like this kind of blues. It's raw.

Some blues purists might not consider that a blues song because it's not a strict I IV V. It's kind of a heavy radio song. But that's hot stuff. That's my kind of blues. This friend of mine always used to play that song. He killed it every time. It was awesome. We are going to enter this into our song list immediately. We were going to learn it a couple months ago; we haven't yet but we definitely got to do it now. In fact, give me this tape.

# ROBBEN FORD

**“Killing Floor”**
The Electric Flag
*A Long Time Comin’*
**ROBBEN:** I haven’t heard this in years. This brings back a lot of memories. When this record came out, it was my breakfast, lunch and dinner. It’s a pleasure to hear it again. I never heard the original song by Howlin’ Wolf. This music sounded completely new and fresh when I first heard it. It still sounds fresh. It could come out today. This is exactly what I did on *Talk to Your Daughter*—take old blues songs and revamp them. This is an obvious example of where the idea to do such a thing came from.

Mike Bloomfield was my first guitar hero, and probably the only one that I ever emulated to the point where I used to sound a lot like him. I never got into his Indian raga thing, that funny little scale he used to play like he does on “Another Country” from this album. But prior to hearing the Paul Butterfield Blues Band, with Mike Bloomfield on guitar, I’d never heard anybody playing so much guitar. When I heard that first Butterfield record, that’s when I knew what I wanted to do. I think I was 14. I have a real good ear, so I could hear this pretty quickly and kind of emulate it real fast. Emotionally, I could identify with it.

**“Miles”**
Miles Davis
*Milestones*
**ROBBEN:** For the last three years I’ve gone through this period of listening to old Miles Davis records. I’m in love with the man. He is the most inspirational musician of my life. It was a wonderful thing growing up listening to what he did in the ’60s. I love that music and dug it all the way up to *Bitches Brew.* At that point I stopped listening. I didn’t find Miles records after *Bitches Brew* to mean anything to me. I would always go back to *Miles Smiles*, *Miles in the Sky*, and *Nefertiti*, *Sorcerer*. Those are wonderful records.

At some point I realized that there were these older Miles Davis records that I never paid attention to. I had heard some of them, like *’Round About Midnight*, *Four & More* and *My Funny Valentine.* Those are actually from the early ’60s. There was all this stuff before with Red Garland, Paul Chambers, Philly Joe Jones and Cannonball Adderley. For the last three years I’ve been listening to that stuff a lot. These players are the greatest improvisers of their day.

This song is a classic. I don’t have anything to say about it in particular. It’s more the musicians and the style they are playing in. There are a lot of different phases in Miles Davis’ music. You can pick up one record and not relate to it, pick up another and love it. It depends on what you’re listening to. What I love about it, however, is the range of emotional expression in terms of dynamics and space, playing from the softest ballad to the most burning complex tune.

The man is an artist, a musician. He’s not a showman. If somebody is a flashy guitar player I’m impressed, but I’m not going to listen to it for very long. When you’re talking about someone like Miles Davis, it’s going to require a little bit of subtlety and attention to detail, and appreciation of space and emotional breadth. It’s a much broader picture.

**“Help Me”**
Joni Mitchell
*Court and Spark*
**ROBBEN:** This was the third tune of our set when I was working with Joni on the road. The album had just come out. The band was great and had a great time on stage. The *Miles of Aisles* record is one of my prized musical experiences to have on record. If you’re talking about pop artists and recording, this album is a jewel in the rough. It has great writing; she is singing like a bird.

I was not a part of the *Court and Spark* record, but I understand they had a lot of trouble making it. It seems to be a product of many things. You have some of the most beautiful accompaniments on it. I never paid a lot of attention to accompanying guitarists. I was listening to Coltrane and Miles. I learned to accompany over the years, finding myself in situations where I had to come up with something.

This is wonderful accompaniment. For most of the album I believe it’s Larry Carlton. Larry is one of the most amazing accompanists alive today. He is probably the best. You certainly hear a tune artist at work there. Everyone on the record is an artist. Everybody is creating the right thing for the right moment.

**“Please Don’t Feel Bad”**
Steve Smith and Vital Information
*Fiafiaga (Celebration)*
**ROBBEN:** That’s some of the most refreshing guitar playing I’ve heard since I can’t remember when. Great playing, real musical and fiery. Frank [Gambale] is playing his butt off. It’s musical, which is unusual to hear from guitar players these days. It has a real nice combination of blues kinds of lines and much more sophisticated harmony. He tied it all together really well. It flowed so well. I’m impressed. There are some interesting chord changes in

there and he was making a lot of music out of it. There aren't too many people who can play like that.

**"Demons"**
Gregg Allman
*Just Before the Bullets Fly*
**ROBBEN:** The opening sounds like Larry Carlton. No, it's somebody playing a Les Paul. Sounds like a hell of a guitar player. I really enjoyed it. The guy is not playing any wrong notes; he's got a great sound, a lot of control over what he's doing. He's different; he doesn't just sound like his influences. He's got his own thing going on there. Two thumbs up. I just heard a different Gregg Allman cut on the radio yesterday and dug the guitar player. I thought, "Wow, who is this guy?"
**JOHN:** It's Dan Toler
**ROBBEN:** I'm going to get this for the guitar player. The guy is fun to hear.

**"Voodoo Thing"**
Colin James
*Colin James*
**ROBBEN:** It sounds like a real good guitar player. This isn't something that appeals to me quite as much as other things, only because it's a little rougher than I like to hear. I don't hear a lot of musicality in it. I don't mean that as a putdown. It's real raw and gutsy. It doesn't sound good to me. I accentuate the word *sound* because it's really that. It's not real dimensional.

**"Finish What Ya Started"**
Van Halen
*OU812*
**ROBBEN:** I don't listen to much rock, but I love the feel and what Eddie is playing. It's not loud. It's a groovin' thing. He's a great guitar player and it's a great concert band. I've not listened to him

much in the past. Actually, *Diver Down* is the only Eddie Van Halen I've heard. I like this a lot. I didn't expect to hear this from him.

**JOHN:** How do you get beyond playing clichés in your soloing?

**ROBBEN:** There's no problem with clichés; they are fine. But you need to take them in, so they are part of you as opposed to you are playing this lick, this thing that came from outside that you happen to put on like a hat. It's got to come in and become your lick. It's just like language. It's identical to having a conversation. You learn how to talk before you learn how to read.

# RORY GALLAGHER

**"Tube Snake Boogie"**
Z.Z. Top
*El Loco*
**RORY:** It has a Creedence sort of feel, with an almost Dave Edmunds production. It could be the T-Birds. It could be the Blasters. I thought it was Thorogood at the start. The feel is nice. It's "Music to go," as Nick Lowe would say. Two different rhythms going with the drums and guitars is nice; it's blazing and sleazy at the same time. I like this kind of stuff. The guitar sound is nice. I like that distorted edge.
**JOHN:** It's ZZ Top
**RORY:** They normally don't have that mix in their records. The lyrics aren't anything to write home about. I like to take the lyrics one step beyond that. My only criticism is that I don't like that style of drum mix. But I like the ambiance of the song. I like records that don't sound like they were recorded in a studio. I like things that sound like they were recorded in somebody's garage.

**"Little Wing"**
Jimi Hendrix
*The Jimi Hendrix Concerts*
**RORY:** That's a side of Hendrix that I like. It's often overlooked. It's the quiet side. It sounds a little like Curtis Mayfield phrasing. Hendrix was the only one who could pull that stuff off with the

wah, the Uni-Vibe, and the tremolo bar and keep the number right down on the floor. The vocal is good. It's almost sounds like an overdub, but it isn't. It's like listening to Django; you almost can't judge it. You have to say it's either brilliant or just great. I'd say this is somewhere in between. It was beautiful. Tuning the guitar down a semitone gives it a low rumble. Van Halen does that tuning as well. The Beatles used to tune down there for numbers like "Please Please Me," where there were such high vocal parts.

**Checking Out**
Allan Holdsworth
*I.O.U.*
**RORY:** A Stevie Wonder-ish arrangement. It could be Jack Bruce and Robin Trower. Maybe it's Allan Holdsworth. Whoever it is, it's nice. It's fusion-ish, but it still has a bit of steel in it. The guitar playing is flashy, but still in the pocket. He's got all the tricks, but he keeps the bravado part of it in check. I didn't like the ending at all. I hate science fiction ending.

**"Farther Up the Road"**
Eric Clapton and Jeff Beck
*The Secret Policeman's Other Ball*
**RORY:** Is this a bootleg performance? It's obviously Eric Clapton. It sounded clumsy. The drumming was awful. If it's a radio thing or a bootleg you can't preach about it.
**JOHN:** It was a real recording.
**RORY:** Clapton's voice sounded all right. The guitar solo was spiky and to the point. He's never anything less than clear and to the point. On another night you'd get a better performance.
**JOHN:** Did you hear another guitarist?
**RORY:** I did. It was like the guy came up and jammed. It wasn't Albert Lee. I tried hard to guess who it was, but the guy must have been playing a Gibson. It wasn't a Fender.
**JOHN:** It was Jeff Beck

**RORY:** Are you kidding me? Was this *The Secret Policeman's Other Ball?* Then we're judging guys who have four tunes to play that night. Under those circumstances, I wouldn't claim to do any better. Who was playing drums?

**JOHN:** Simon Phillips.

**RORY:** Simon is fine on those Pete Townshend albums where there's a lot of room for playing around. When it comes to blues, you have to be so careful. With the exception of Ginger Baker, you can't put 17 tom-tom rolls in there. You can't put a synthesizer in the blues. I didn't write the book, but there are certain things that irritate me if they are not right in this sort of stylized blues. On a good night, Eric Clapton is a cauldron of fire. Intensity is his talent, more than any technical ability.

# BILLY GIBBONS (ZZ TOP)

**"Mannish Boy"**
Muddy Waters
*Hard Again*
**BILLY:** Muddy with Johnny. I need to comment immediately. This was the real heart and soul restoring that '40s and '50s golden era sensibilities to blues. We should have all known it would have taken a guy like Johnny Winter, who had lamented the absence of that music for so long that he himself not only learned how but took it to the streets and said, Hey, this is what it sounds like. And then go back and find one of the originators and lend, shall we say, a retrospective hand of support, saying, Let's restore what I feel may be important to this kind of music. And we're hearing it. This is a great track.

**"Cry Baby"**
Janis Joplin
*Pearl*
**BILLY:** What a great song, Janis Joplin doing "Cry Baby." I remember when she did this. It was really the first indicator of where she had come from. The original track by Garnet Mimms was a big hit in the Gulf Coast, where we were raised. The original Garnet Mimms version had the most interesting guitar figure in it. As it faded out, the guy did a liquid trill that followed the vocal line. It was one of the great Gulf Coast songs that had neat lead guitar.

Hearing this version by Janis reinforces just how much the Gulf Coast thing influenced us all. She had a choice to do a lot of different kinds of material and she chose that one. She probably told her guitar player to go out and learn this. It was a great one. Most of her stuff was so right on. How can you slight Janis for what she did? She was gifted with that grainy voice that made her so listenable.

**"I Smell a Rat"**
Buddy Guy
*Stone Crazy!*

**BILLY:** Whoever it is, I'd like to meet him. This is ferocious. Is that Buddy Guy? I didn't recognize him until the end. I haven't heard that. Somehow, I missed that one, but I'll stick to my first comment. It's pretty ferocious. I should have known Buddy Guy.

I was with Dusty and Frank and we saw Buddy Guy playing. I can't remember where it was. It was awhile back. He looked with great mystery at his own guitar, at his own playing. He just exuded this sensibility or this feeling like, How am I doing this? It really drew you in as one musician to another. We were right there saying, How is he doing that? During the course of the evening, he must have broken five or six strings and didn't even slow down. It didn't faze him; he just turned it up. Maybe it's about attitude. If you don't have any strings, you can't play much, but you can certainly look like, How did I do that?

**JOHN:** Artists often say to their fans, "If you want to learn about me, listen to my influences." If they are not ready to jump right to Muddy Waters, where else should they start?

**BILLY:** So, you've got a guitar and you've just opened the case and you're looking at the first set of six strings that you've ever laid your eyes on. You've just stepped off the train and you're looking for the blues. Through the marvels of the medium of recorded music, one could easily beat a path to Jimmy Reed and there you'll find the most cohesive, well-structured I-IV-V chord change that could really be the backbone of what most people recognize now as blues. Anything by Jimmy Reed will do, and that's as good a primer as you could ask for. From there when you speak of blues you really speak of Muddy Waters. Move from Mississippi to Chicago so the early Chess recordings of Muddy Waters, Howlin' Wolf, Jimmy Rogers and Elmore James. It's quite easy for those that are intimate with Muddy Waters' music or Jimmy Reed's music to see where we came from.

**JOHN:** If people like ZZ Top they will like Jimmy Reed.

**BILLY:** Yeah, definitely. It's as simple a form as you could ask for. It's a step out of the country blues and it really hits that middle ground.

**JOHN:** Is the blues evolving?

**BILLY:** Let me borrow a Keith Richards quote. He said it may be the same three chords, but let's just figure out a new way to present it. Just about the time you think that it's all been done, then you say, What about this way? So there is perhaps the possibility of endless variations on a theme that doesn't necessarily need improvement.

**JOHN:** But it does change over time.

**BILLY:** We can be bold enough to say there is a certain fairness when you allow blues to be a changing art form. Yes, there's a blues museum, but they leave the back door open so the fresh air can continue to breeze through. Let's lean on blues as that comfortable cornerstone which we can spring forward from and anything goes.

# DAVID GILMOUR (PINK FLOYD)

**"Once Upon a Time in the West"**
Dire Straits
*Communiqué*
**DAVID:** Dire Straits. "Once Upon a Time" is not one of my favorite songs of theirs, actually. It just doesn't seem to have that spark to me. He has come on in leaps and bounds. He's got a lovely, refreshing guitar style. He brought back something that seems to have gone astray in guitar players. He plays great on this song. I just don't think the actual song itself is as strong as some of the other ones. I mean "Sultans of Swing" is a classic. I like "Romeo and Juliet," and the live album they just put out is brilliant. I've seen them live a couple of times. I find brilliance a hard thing to pin down. What makes something good or what makes something really good is hard to say. I think he's a great guitar player and a great writer.

**"Tin Pan Alley"**
Stevie Ray Vaughan
*Couldn't Stand the Weather*
**DAVID:** It's the blues. What can you say? Is that B.B. King? It sounds a little like B.B., but very much that style. I can't myself be a purist like that. I like listening to that but I would not ever be able to not throw in something that was completely outside of the blues

formula, if you like. Not that SRV doesn't either. It sounds a little too formularized, slightly formularized blues.

**JOHN:** The heart of what you do as a lead player is as a blues guitarist.

**DAVID:** That's pretty much in there, yeah, but with no rules attached. I'm not going to stick with any of it because it feels like it ought to be there. Yes, I am an incessant dabbler. I have no qualms whatsoever about using any guitar or effect that happens to take my fancy at any given moment. I don't know what I'm looking for half the time.

# BUDDY GUY

**"Mojo Hand (Part 1)"**
Lightnin' Hopkins
*Mojo Hand: Anthology*
**BUDDY:** Lightnin' Hopkins was the first guitarist I heard who could make me forget about my playmates. I was born so far in the country I didn't know what electric lights were until I was just about in my teens, so we didn't have radios and things like that. When I finally heard Lightnin', it was just like, This is *it*, man. You guys go out to play by yourselves now because I've got to hear this.

We did have an opportunity on a Christmas Day to go somewhere where somebody may have a radio and an old windup phonograph. This was special, because it was a little bit before B.B King. B.B. King and other people who learned a lot from Lightnin' will tell you it's something about your guitar playing and your voice that can be special. And the way Lightnin' played, well, that voice and his guitar had something in common that's impossible to reproduce unless it's him. You'd have to go get him out of his grave and say, "Hey Lightnin', you've got to come here and do this over again because I haven't found anybody else to do that yet."

But the tone of his guitar and the tone of his voice is something that is not ever going to be redone again. It relates to his guitar and the things he learned in the country and the country type of blues that he played. He was way before all this modern technology we've got with the guitars and amplifiers and all that. The main thing was the truthfulness of what he is doing. Because I know as a youngster, when I was listening to him, I learned that there was no future in playing music; you just play it because you love it.

**"Blue Guitar"**
Earl Hooker
*Blues Masters, Vol. 2: Postwar Chicago Blues*
**BUDDY:** This guy here was similar to what I went through. He was ignored a lot in Chicago, but he played slide on one album with Muddy [Waters]. When I arrived in Chicago, for six or seven weeks nobody knew who I was because I didn't run around with the guitar players, walking in to play.

I saw Earl Hooker, and the first thing I did was hand him my slide. I said, "After I saw you play the slide, I didn't want to even have one in my pocket." I have never seen anybody play a slide like him. He'd never take his slide off his finger, but he would start playing the same damn thing that we were playing fingering on the guitar. And he was great on that.

That's him on the original Junior Wells song "Messing with the Kid." Nowhere else could you find a guy who would not retune his guitar and take that slide and play the same thing I'm playing, and still have that slide on his little finger. Man, that's when we used to have the fun. He would tell me, "You can jump around on the stage all you want; I put that slide on and it will sit you down." I would say, "You surely will." And he did, on many nights. When I saw him play, I would do just like I do with B.B. and Muddy, when he was alive. When they play, I listen.

**"Killing Floor"**
Howling Wolf
*The Real Folk Blues*
**BUDDY:** This is one of those sessions that Willie Dixon, Wolf, and Leonard [Chess] had. They had high hopes on this song. I

think this could be one of the longest sessions they had. Leonard was the type of guy who could hum the stuff that he wanted someone to play. That's like I am today, and that's the way I learned how to play.

I think they had tried this song for a night, maybe two nights in a row and they decided to call my house. Dixon called the house and said, "Come down here. Leonard wants you to hear something." I got there and he hummed me this bass pattern. And I walked in there and I played it. They would call you MF's and he said, "This MF knows how to play exactly what I been asking for." And I did this whole pattern for the Wolf on that thing in less than three minutes. They say, "That MF will sit back and listen."

We cut that in less than an hour after they had been listening for two or three days. I was so proud that they got me out of the bed to come play; I didn't need money. It didn't have anything to do with it. The union would give you a little check for making the albums then. I didn't even want to see that. I'd just say, "Wow, another chance to play with the Howlin' Wolf."

**"I Just Want to Make Love to You"**
Muddy Waters
*The Best of Muddy Waters*

**BUDDY:** Well, you know that's some of my favorite stuff there. That's Little Walter and Muddy Waters. I don't know if Jimmy Rogers is on that. But they are the guys who changed the face of the earth with the amplifier and the harmonica and guitar.

Willie Dixon writes unforgettable stuff. That record there, I go to the stage right now and start singing that. Young people recognize it. I don't know if they recognize it from Muddy or someone else who has done it. But that's Willie Dixon writing, Muddy Waters playing.

So many British groups have redone Muddy, the Wolf and Sonny Boy's stuff. I'm very proud of the super rock groups who went back, like Led Zeppelin, and Clapton in the Cream days, and kept these guys' names alive.

Today we are the best of friends, and they know how I feel about what they did for me and all of these great old blues players, some of them who are not around to hear this. If there's such thing as smiling down from heaven, they are smiling down from heaven, because as long as I'm alive I'm going to be doing songs like this to the best that I can. I will be doing it to let you, your children, my children, and my grandchildren know that this was a part of Buddy Guy. This is what kept Buddy Guy's spirit alive.

**"Déjà Voodoo"**

Kenny Wayne Shepherd

*Ledbetter Heights*

**BUDDY:** I know who that is, but I can't get the name on that one. Oh, man, I like that. That's a Jimi Hendrix/Stevie Ray Vaughan tone that we all had. Most all of the tones—when Leo Fender was around—were similar to this big fat tone. All those things are collected now, and you almost have to go back to Stevie and Eric and all these guys who could collect them. A lot of Japanese people collect all those guitars and amps that got that tone. You can't get them much anymore. You see them every once in a while. That's the tone that I came to Chicago with, but then they stole all of my '55, '56 Strats. That Strat will give you this tone on almost any amplifier. We didn't have all the different things until the '60s, when CBS and everybody else got those amplifiers and made a rat race out of them. And, to me, they lost their tone.

**JOHN:** That's 18-year-old Kenny Wayne Shepherd.

**BUDDY:** You're kidding! He had the Hendrix tone down to a T. When I hear that tone, you always catch me thinking of Jimi. Hendrix was one of the most creative guitar players that I ever heard in my life. It's a shame he's not still with us. I'm going to have to get this because I've got to try to steal some licks from him. Tell him I said this song is going to follow me from now on because I like what I'm hearing.

**"Five Long Years"**
Eric Clapton
*From the Cradle*
**BUDDY:** That's my buddy. Santana popped that on for me and I knew that Eddie Boyd [composer] was going to be very proud of him for doing this song because whatever Eric touches turns to gold. He is one of the greatest guys you'd want to know. I'm very proud to have him as one of my best friends. He made the comment several years ago that I was the greatest guitar player alive. Where I come from, actions speak louder than words. I think he is. Eric and B.B. King are the only two guitar players that I know that can just stand there. They don't have to tap their feet or nothing to make you listen. Sometimes I have to jump off the stage and run around the audience and tap you on the shoulder and say, "Here I am."

I did "Five Long Years" on *Damn Right, I've Got the Blues*. Eric was on that album with me. I was glad to see him play this. Anything he does, the disc jockeys, the media, and everybody else will play it. This album went to Number One on the charts. I would like to see the major radio stations and whoever played it let their listeners know exactly where it came from. It didn't come from Buddy Guy. I told Eddie Boyd, just before he died, that I was going to do this song. He said, "Anything you do will help me. I'm here now, I'm sinking, I'm old and I'm kind of sick. That little money will help." And wherever he is today, I'm sure he was smiling at Eric when Eric did it.

I listen to Eric more than I do anybody else now. If I play an Eric or Stevie song I get criticized by journalists. But when they play mine, they never get criticized. I'm talking about black and white, so I pay that no mind. I've learned to live with that because I love what Eric can do, man. These guys ask me the same stupid question a thousand times. "Can a white guy play the blues?" They say he can't play it because he has not lived the blues and all that.

Man, that's not true. You've got five fingers and two hands. You can do it.

**"Pride and Joy"**
Stevie Ray Vaughan
*The Unplugged Collection, Volume One*
**BUDDY:** Stevie Ray Vaughan. Irreplaceable. Guys like him only come once in a lifetime. Being from Texas, he opened that door up for blues, for myself, and for a lot more people. Stevie Ray had a skeleton key to the closet where they had us all locked in, and he opened the door and let us all out. And then he went back and got my songs and quite a few more people's songs and brought them out and said, "This is what this is all about." He told the world where Buddy Guy was, Robert Cray, Lonnie Mack, or whoever he wanted. He was just a true guy.

## KIRK HAMMETT, JOE SATRIANI

**"Tube Snake Boogie"**
ZZ Top
*El Loco*
**JOE:** I love ZZ Top. I always have, even though I don't have very many Top records. Every time I hear the stuff, I hear great ideas behind their songs. The way they approach key changes, where they put solos, how long they are, the ensemble parts and the subjects get to me. It's funny yet it's serious, and the guitar playing is never excessive. The sense of rhythm is always there. All my chromosomes stand on end when I play boogie.
**KIRK:** When I started playing guitar, I was under the influence of my older brother and his album collection, which consisted of stuff like Cream, Zeppelin and Hendrix. When I read interviews, they'd always talk about older blues people, and for a while, when I started playing, I was playing shuffles and boogie stuff. Then I discovered ZZ Top and Lynyrd Skynyrd, and for two years straight that's all I would listen to. Heavy metal has a lot to do with the blues.
**JOHN:** Have you heard Megadeth do Jeff Beck's version of "I Ain't Superstitious"?
**KIRK:** No, but I would do covers of Jeff Beck's covers. "Let Me Love You Baby" was the first guitar solo I ever tried to figure out. I played it horribly.
**JOHN:** Do you ever just jam anymore?
**KIRK:** Jamming with someone helps your playing a lot more than

just playing by yourself. Jamming is the time to pursue other outside interests. I am heavily into the blues. Buddy Guy, Albert King, B.B. King, of course the Vaughan brothers. I just picked up Magic Slim. He rips. Robert Johnson is incredible. Son House is too. When Clarence “Gatemouth” Brown picks up a violin and plays blues licks, I feel like crying all the way home.

I play Mississippi Delta blues style, slide, some Hendrixy stuff. One time I played “Voodoo Chile” for an hour. One night when I really drunk, I sang “I’m a Man.” Howlin’ Wolf wrote some pretty heavy riffs. “Smokestack Lightning” is the riff everyone knows. Back then it was considered dirty and lowdown. It was the devil’s music. I’ve seen flyers that say Metallica is the devil’s music. If you turned it up and played it aggressively, “Smokestack Lightening” is basically a heavy metal song.

# WARREN HAYNES
# (THE ALLMAN BROTHERS BAND, GOV'T MULE)

**"The Brother"**
Robben Ford
*Robben Ford & the Blue Line*
**WARREN:** It's *Blue Line* right? That's the one he did for SRV and Jimmy. I've been a fan of Robben Ford's playing since 1974 when I first heard him on the Tom Scott *Tom Cat* album. I think he was real young when he did that. Since then I've heard him play with everybody from George Harrison to Joni Mitchell, Miles Davis, Charlie Musselwhite.

I love Robben's playing and always have loved his playing. I'm glad he's doing a bluesy type thing, although I think my favorite stuff that he ever did was in the kind of bluesy jazz kind of stuff. When I was kid, I even had the record *Schizophonic*. That's the one where he's playing sax and guitar.

I think it's always been hard for Robben to make a record that he was satisfied that record companies were satisfied with too. A lot of people have that same dilemma, especially musicians as talented as he is. When you can do so many kinds of things, there's always somebody telling you what they think you should do. I think one of his problems—obviously it's not a problem—is his versatility. He can play so many different types of music convincingly that sometimes it can be hard to make the decision which direction to go in. I like him playing bluesy type stuff but I always like him playing jazzy stuff too.

**JOHN:** Let's listen to some more of the track.

**WARREN:** Of all the cats capable of playing jazz and jazz-oriented music, he is the only one that to me can be really convincing in a straight blues or straight rock kind of setting. Most cats that are good enough to play in that jazz sort of arena don't have the straight-ahead feel and the emotional thing that Robben has in that kind of respect.

I've always loved his playing. His tone is always great. I remember I was in Sterling Sound mastering my record and I heard the newest one; I heard it coming out of one of the other mastering studios and I turned my head and said, That's got to be Robben Ford. It was the tone and the playing. I walked in and listened to it for a minute. Like I say, I've always loved his playing and am glad to see him making records in any direction he chooses—because he is convincing in all of them.

**"Miles"**

Miles Davis

*Milestones*

**WARREN:** This song is called "Miles." I probably have more Miles Davis records than any other artist in my collection. Cannonball is playing alto. Coltrane playing tenor is one of the scariest things I've ever heard in my life. Not to mention Miles' genius and Red Garland and Jimmy Cobb and Paul Chambers. I think that's who it is.

Cannonball [Adderley] is like the most underrated soloist of all time in my opinion. He had something so special. It's like what would be interpreted a few years later as soul sax, like Junior Walker and King Curtis. Cannonball had a little bit of that before anybody else did. Everybody says he is just playing from the Charlie Parker school. No, he graduated from there and went way somewhere else. His control of the instrument is just amazing.

I think you could listen to Miles Davis for 100 years and still not learn half of what you're supposed to learn. The thing is, with me, when I started out, I was a guitar freak. But in the past ten years I've probably been more influenced by horns then by guitars. Just because of the melodic structures they tend to play and the parameters they tend to play in, the variance in tone is so different than the way a guitar player will approach it. That's what I can learn form, adapting other instruments to my own.

**JOHN:** Is there a song where you were imitating a horn player?

**WARREN:** On "Kind of Bird" on the *Shades of Two Worlds* album, we cut that song live and my solo, I think, is live on the track. I remember after we got done, Allen Woody coming up to me saying, "That's great, man; you played a sax solo." I thought I kind of did. It was an instrumental I wrote with Dickey Betts that was a tribute mostly to Charlie Parker, and also to Miles Davis from the *Kind of Blue* record. It was nominated for a Grammy for Best Rock Instrumental Performance. It was one of the things I'm most proud of that I've done with the Allman Brothers Band.

But that song not only has my solo and Dickey's solo, but a lot of the melodic structure is like a horn feel. It was great. We played it on the *Tonight Show* with the *Tonight Show* band and the horns played the melody. Dickey and I kind of grinned because we knew that's what we were writing anyway, a horn melody, just interpreting it for guitar.

**"The Calling"**

Yes

*Talk*

**WARREN:** I've always been a big Yes fan. I'm probably more of a fan of the old band than I am of the new band, but I think most people feel that way about the bands that they've loved for so many years. That's quite an impressive track. It's the first time I've heard it. Really cool solo, really nice section in the middle. It sounds sort of like Mahavishnu [Orchestra] meets Kansas with all the odd bars and stuff.

Trevor Rabin is an amazing guitar player. I saw him play one time and he is incredible. I'm a huge Steve Howe fan and always was. I just think there is something quirky about Steve Howe and the way he plays that is so hard to duplicate. You can learn what he plays but you can't play it the way he played it. He has this Jimmy Page thing, although he is more of an accomplished technical guitar player then Page. He has this sloppiness that is so hard to match.

It's funny, people probably think I'm crazy when I say this, but the Allman Brothers combined blues and rock and jazz as three of their major influences. And if you took out the blues and inserted classical music, that's kind of what Yes did—classical and rock and jazz combined in a way. It's very similar. Both bands had a bass player that played more than the average bass player played. They played counterpoint and melodic lines. The bands have nothing in common, but I've always thought that there was kind of a similar approach in the way they mixed their ingredients.

I have always been a big Yes fan and I find myself listening to the old stuff, but I don't listen a whole lot to the new stuff. The new stuff is more backbeat oriented. I am a backbeat guy, but my favorite Yes stuff was when they were more into the odd time signatures. I like this.

**"Statesboro Blues"**
Taj Mahal
*Taj Mahal*

**WARREN:** Taj Mahal doing "Statesboro Blues." That's where the Allman Brothers Band got their version, which is the definitive version. To my knowledge, it's Jesse Ed Davis playing slide, and Ry Cooder playing rhythm guitar, which is pretty amazing. We had the great pleasure in Telluride a few years ago to be on the same bill with Taj, and he came out and did "Statesboro Blues" with us.

A small percentage of the fans actually knew the hipness factor of that—that he had done it before the Brothers, and that is where they got it from.

Gregg jokes around, half joking about Duane being sick and him bringing him a bottle of Coricidin and a Taj Mahal record. Apparently, there was a time when Duane was very infatuated with Jesse Ed's playing and influenced a lot by it. I remember reading an interview where Duane made the statement that hearing Ry Cooder play slide is what made him want to play slide guitar. I thought that was a cool statement because both of those guys opened the door for slide guitar players.

I love Taj Mahal and I love that old stuff. That track in particular was great. It's amazing, Duane copped a lot of the licks, not so much the tone and the phrasing but some of the melodic notes. A lot are the same as in "Done Somebody Wrong," from Elmore James' version. It's the same kind of approach. What if I played this with my approach and my tone but played the same kind of stuff? It's a great way of seeing the natural progression from one step to another.

I played with Taj at the Wetlands one night here in New York. The owner of the club was a friend of mine. The manger, at the time, was a friend of mine. He said, "Would you like to play with Taj?" I said, "I don't have a guitar." He said, "Well, if he's up for it, maybe he'll play piano and you can play his acoustic." Taj was playing solo by himself. The manager said, "Why don't you do 'Statesboro Blues?' " I said, "I don't have a slide." He said, "Maybe he's got one?" We'll see. They called me up. Taj said, "What do you want to play?" I said, "He recommended 'Statesboro Blues.' " "Okay, you got a slide?" I look in my pocket and I've got this little Bic lighter, not the big one, the small one. Taj hands me his acoustic with real low action. He starts playing piano in G and the "Statesboro Blues" we do is in D. He plays this boogie-woogie and I'm over here with the Bic lighter playing bam-bam-bam. It had nothing to do with "Statesboro Blues." It was hilarious.

**"Loser"**
Beck
*Mellow Gold*

**WARREN:** I don't listen to mainstream music as much as I listen to other eclectic music, I guess. I've heard that song a few times; I realize it's Beck and the song "Loser." The chorus is kind of hooky and the song is kind of timely, humorous and poignant. It's not really something that I would find myself listening to, but I do appreciate a lot of the new types of music that are coming out. I enjoy more the ones that incorporate real bands. From what I hear, his touring experience is not like a real band.

It's a pretty cool song, kind of came out of the blue. You pointed out it has the whole acoustic slide part in there, which is kind of cool. I haven't heard anything else by him, so I really have no idea what to expect.

**JOHN:** In some ways it's back porch 1994.

**WARREN:** Yeah, I know what you mean; it's got the acoustic part in there that is very folky.

**"Nobody Hears Me Crying"**
Dave Hole
*Working Overtime*

**WARREN:** That's Dave Hole, right? I've heard a little bit of his stuff but not a whole lot. Very good slide player. I like the real wide vibrato; it's similar to the vibrato that Ry Cooder uses sometimes, like on the *Crossroads* soundtrack. It's kind of what it reminds me of a little bit, in the scene where they are cutting heads at the end of the movie *Crossroads*. It's the real wide vibrato that Ry is using on the slide. I use that kind of vibrato a lot myself to separate from the more narrow quick vibrato. Just to get two or three different variations. This is cool, I dig it. It's barroom blues. It's got a very smoky kind of atmosphere to it.

The song didn't hit me so much; I was listening more for the guitar playing. It's hard for me to go much beyond that only hearing it for the first time that way. But everything I heard about him I thought was good. I don't know how this track compares to the rest of the record. It just seems very kind of stock barroom shuffle. Not in a bad way; maybe I would like to hear it go into something a little different.

**"Daddy Long Legs"**
Johnny Gale
*Gale Force*

**WARREN:** Eric Clapton? When I first heard it I thought it was Clapton; I don't think it is. He is playing more aggressively than Eric plays these days, but it is so reminiscent of old Clapton—Cream Clapton but with his later tones, with the Strat tone. I'm not sure who it is; they are playing their ass off.

I'm focusing on the guitar playing and the guitar player is very good. Very much paying homage to a few different people, more of the early Clapton than anybody else, but it's very confident, very aggressive in-your-face guitar playing. But very reminiscent of old Clapton playing.

Clapton was my first guitar hero. I forget sometimes how much I learned from Eric Clapton. In the formative years, that's so important. The first few years that you're playing, you digest so much stuff. I was so into Clapton the first several years that sometimes I don't realize how much of that stayed with me.

**JOHN:** This strikes a chord with you.

**WARREN:** Definitely. I don't know who it is playing; I didn't recognize the tone. It's a Strat tone thing. I dig it. It kind of caught me by surprise just because I was expecting it to be some live Clapton cut.

**JOHN:** This is Johnny Gale, a New York blues guy.

**WARREN:** He is playing good, man. Cool. Good playing.

## JUSTIN HAYWARD (THE MOODY BLUES)

**"Good Morning Little School Girl"**
Eric Clapton (with the Yardbirds)
*Crossroads*

**JUSTIN:** When was it recorded, '62? It was exactly the kind of thing I would have done just before the Beatles came out—when you know there's something just around the corner that's going to be really good, but you can't quite put your finger on it. It sounds quite English. I know "Good Morning Little School Girl" is an American sentiment. But everybody in England sang with an American accent until the Beatles, so it doesn't matter. Everyone's heroes were Americans. Great Britain never really had any rock 'n' roll heroes. Maybe Tommy Steele, but he was like a parrot of Elvis. It reminds me of my own playing in some social club or school dance.

**JOHN:** That was early Eric Clapton.

**JUSTIN:** Was it really? What band? [The Yardbirds] It's not Eric singing. It doesn't really sound like Eric playing guitar either. If that band had stayed together, they would have become like Manfred Mann, that kind of thing. Eric Clapton, I wouldn't have put it there at all. The guitar solo was like from a different record. When you told me there was to be a guitar solo, I expected one of those funny sort of Beach Boys takeoffs of Chuck Berry in there. But it wasn't; it was quite clear and very melodic.

**JOHN:** Were you influenced by Clapton?

**JUSTIN:** I can't actually say I was. He was only an influence in so much as we supported Cream on several dates on their farewell tour of America. It was '68. I always adored his playing, but I never considered myself to be that kind of player. There was never anybody coming to a Moody Blues concert to watch my left hand.

# JEFF HEALEY

**"Struttin' with Some Barbeque"**
Louis Armstrong and His Hot Five
*The Smithsonian Collection of Classic Jazz*
**JEFF:** Twenty points out of ten for picking a work of genius. I know this record from start to finish. I can even tell you the date—December 9, 1927. It's the Armstrong Hot Five with "Struttin' with Some Barbeque." The tune was written by pianist Lil Armstrong, who of course was Louis's wife at that time

I can't think of any Hot Five record that doesn't have some amount of merit. Now, Lord knows, Louis did a handful of things that are not great tunes. They were just thrown at him to do what he wanted. But this being a composition within that little pickup group was fantastic. And this is a tune that—ironically you pulled it out—that sticks in my mind constantly.

I always make the point to beginning musicians that you really have to listen to what other instrumentalists are doing. What Armstrong does on this solo is just a great musically inventive solo. The fact that it's played on a trumpet is trivial. If it were played on a guitar, it's very difficult. If it's played on a saxophone, it's difficult. It's difficult on a piano. It covers a whole wide range of two and a half octaves and it's always energetic with the right dynamics. It's just a perfect record.
**JOHN:** Is there a link between Louis Armstrong and what you play as a guitarist?

**JEFF:** And what a lot of people play. Armstrong was and is the inventor in many ways of the whole improvisational game, that has been picked up by instrumentalist from then on. It just so happens that the rock 'n' roll music genre popularized the guitar as the front instrument.

When you got into people like Jimi Hendrix, Eric Clapton and Jeff Beck, they realized what was missing in rock 'n' roll was improvisation and lots of it. They just sort of capitalized on that whole improvisation medium through the guitar. That's where that all comes from, but it really stems back to Armstrong's complete concept of improvisation through a solo. People before Armstrong improvised little breaks of a bar, but very little, not full 32-bar solos.

The one thing that Armstrong maybe subconsciously did was show the coalition between his voice and his trumpet. You've got a musical instrument and a vocal instrument, which is creating music, which is a little more understood to the average public. But that the two mirrored each other. Take the trumpet away from Louis's lips and he would probably sing the same phrase at that time. It's just the phrase that hit him, which he was able to create either vocally or with the trumpet.

**"Since I Met You Baby"**
Gary Moore (with B.B. King)
*After Hours*
**JEFF:** It's a track I haven't heard. It's certainly an interesting combination. It's that blend of the old with the new. One of the main differences that is striking to a novice is just the difference in sound. Gary Moore is far more reliant on the distortion aspect and the reaction of the pickup to amp, which a lot of us, myself included, are very guilty of falling victim to. It's sort of what you come up on. Whereas B.B. is from that school where you had to make the notes happen and the feeling come out solely with the hands.

You were relying on very primitive equipment when it came to electronic equipment as far as amps or guitars. I have yet to hear a recording that best shows B.B.'s sound. I'm afraid that he is going to be one of those people whose sound can just not be captured in the studio. I say that with all due respect to B.B. because I love him a great deal. He has been very good to me and with me. I consider him a very good acquaintance in the music business.

I am always knocked out to go to a B.B. concert, and especially to have the privilege—and probably the greatest privilege in my life—to sit on stage with B.B. and to listen to him play, listen to that sound that is there on the stage. He has one of those guitar-to-amp sounds that is not overpowering but it's certainly not something that can be overpowered. It completely fills the stage with the same volume whether you are in front of the amp as when you're ten feet to the right or the left of it. It's unbelievable. The microphone just doesn't seem to be able to pick that up.

As I said at the start, this is a real example of the older style, not the old style because B.B. draws a lot, as he will admit, from the Lonnie Johnson school of acoustic playing. Had Lonnie the access to electronic equipment in the '20s it's scary to think how fast music would have progressed.

**JOHN:** Talk a little about this track.

**JEFF:** Okay, I would say not even knowing who the backup musicians are, that maybe they are not quite as soulful as they could be. They are a little more—and a wish I could be more polite about it—but they are a little more white bread bluesy. There's not a lot of guts or balls to it, certainly not the balls of a Howlin' Wolf record or a Muddy Waters record. Those guys had a load of guts in their rhythm section. It might be a little sloppy, but it was sort of grunge blues. There is such a thing as grunge rock. The Seattle sound thing. It was that real kicking out energy for fun stuff.

I think the sad thing about some blues records is the same with listening to people trying to do revival jazz—they never seem to get it right. They always play it as if it's an old style; it's been here, it's gone, and they water it down. We can even go back to the Armstrong stuff. As primitive as the other four players with Armstrong were, there's a real sense of devotion and raw energy there. That's what lacks sometimes; nowadays it tends to get eaten up by production. Which is the good thing I can also say about bands like Pearl Jam or Nirvana or Red Hot Chili Peppers—the production is not huge. They just try to get the sound of the instruments out there. That's a good thing.

You have to have the right musicians around you to back you up, to complement you. You're as good as the other musicians with you when it comes right down to it. It's obvious that Gary Moore has a great respect for what we'll call the blues mentality. I think were he given a more raw production, and musicians who may be a little sloppy but really dig in, he would benefit.

**"Talk to Your Daughter"**

Robben Ford

*Talk to Your Daughter*

**JEFF:** What I liked about that was the production. And I like the rhythm section, particularly the bass and drums together. If you were to get something together like that with what we discussed before, like a Gary Moore, it would be very interesting. I think that Gary Moore maybe has a little more concept of the true soulful delivery than who we just heard as a guitar player. It's okay. I've heard a lot worse.

**JOHN:** It's Robben Ford.

**JEFF:** I have heard a bit of his stuff. He is a good player. That's one thing that frustrates me to a degree. I've certainly come up through the rock era where we did tend to forget a little bit about soul. And slow but sure, for my own satisfaction I tried to get a bit more back to it, but it's a tough thing to do.

It's sort of the problem I have again on the *See the Light* album with the solo on "Confidence Man." I find it unfortunately devoid of soul. I don't dislike this. I've heard a lot worse. I've heard a lot better too. But it's a step in the right direction. Like I said, I'm guilty of it myself. But if you try [to be soulful] you're going to be noticed. So, it's just a matter of immersing yourself in a lot of improvisation from people who I feel have a lot of soul. Like, if I listen to B.B. King, Jack Teagarden, Eric Clapton—who I all think have a lot of soul—you know when you hear what they are doing that they mean it.

**"Rough Boy"**
ZZ Top
*Greatest Hits*
**JEFF:** This is now of course your example of later Billy [Gibbons], because it really is Billy. I have the lowdown but I don't want to comment because I don't want to give away Billy's whole bag. But Billy is the main songwriter, the vocalist and obviously the soloist.
**JOHN:** And sometimes the drummer and bass player.
**JEFF:** You said it, not me. I know because we worked with their producer, Joe Hardy. I know exactly how Billy and Joe have made the records in the last while. It's cool. That's what they are happy doing. I don't knock them for that at all.

A lot of AOR programmers and listeners that I've talked to throughout the years slam ZZ Top for getting into machines. I think that's crap. It's uncalled for and unjustified as in the slamming part. This is a band that has been around since maybe '71 or '72. When you get up to 1983, which is when you start to notice that change, what else were they going to do with three guys? They put horns on their stuff. Dusty had done vocals, and there are great songs with the three of them playing. Where else are you going to go aside from retiring? They obviously didn't want to do that. They are still young guys.

So, your next step is to try and integrate what they do with technology. Technology has to change, or it would be a very boring world in the music industry. Which is why we got into recording digitally. That was a big step for us. It sounds trivial but it was something we had not done. I'm not ashamed to say we sampled a little snippet of guitar. It helped to record with Joe Hardy, who knew the whole digital way of recording. I might just blow on a tune and Joe and I would go through it with him and come out with one second or two seconds of something that was really kind of interesting and might work in many different spots of the whole tune. We sampled it and bring that sample up at the given shot in the tune. What is wrong with that if it adds to the tune? Why not? We did it in "My Kinda Lover," "Cruel Little Number" and "Baby's Looking Hot." But that computer would not work without its programmer's, which was us and Joe.

Getting back to Billy and ZZ, that's sort of what Billy's done. I still like Billy's songwriting and I think he's got some great ideas, which is why I got him involved in "Cruel Little Number." For anybody wants to bash him for getting into electronics, and that kind of thing, the guy still knows how to come up with a certain lyrical idea that's appealing to many people.

**JOHN:** What's your take on "Rough Boy"?

**JEFF:** It's got nice changes; the production between Hardy and Billy is great. It's a good example of Billy's laidback vocals. His guitar playing is great. He's got a very nice sound. He's got a nice feel for just the right notes that fit into that particular pattern that he's playing over. I love Billy. My respect for many musicians might go up and down, but with Billy, I love him.

**"Have You Heard"**

John Mayall & the Bluesbreakers

*Blues Breakers with Eric Clapton*

**JEFF:** I've always been a fan of Clapton as a musician. I came from two backgrounds, jazz and country. A buddy of mine, Rob Quail, was one of the first people to get me into playing and listening to a lot of pure blues. I met Rob Quail when I was 15. He was a couple years older than me. Rob had picked up the guitar about six months before I'd met him, and he'd already become quite an interesting player. He is still thankfully a really good guitar player and has been a great influence to me. But Rob said, "Have you ever heard this John Mayall album? In particular, the song "Have You Heard"? I said no. He said, "You've got to listen to this," and he played it as an example of Eric Clapton's work at that point.

It was obviously Clapton at a very early stage, because Clapton has matured a lot since then as a musician. But what I still like about the tune and about the solo is the youthful raw energy. With "Have You Heard" you hear Clapton at the age of 22. He had not become the well-known singer entertainer. He had nothing to gain or lose. He was just blowing for the sake of blowing. It is to a degree a very rudimentary solo, but it's that youthful energy that sometimes can get lost in music. It's very important to have your days of youthful energy just to let rip and let things fall where they may, without any particular reason or thought process to it. Eric really covers it and it's very emotional.

The amazing thing about that solo was that he was from the London area and I don't believe by that point had made any trips to the U.S. He was relying solely on records of blues players that he had heard, that had come over from the U.S. He was relying on those to get his inspiration and it was remarkable just how quickly a 22-year-old kid tapped into that whole feeling, that whole genre and where he took it from there. Eric is still making great records.

**"Smoking Gun"**

Robert Cray

*Strong Persuader*

**JEFF:** I was made aware of Robert Cray somewhere around 1984 through blues shows in Canada and a couple of people who had heard the albums. He had one, maybe two albums at that point. I thought he was a great singer and I still think Robert has a great voice.

Robert is one of those few examples that we have in music today of a musician who is able to perfectly link his guitar playing and his whole guitar playing style and feel with his vocal style and feel. It's a combination of the two, and a very good combination of the two. They really work well together. Robert isn't one of those flashy guitar players and I don't think he wants to be or tries to be.

The beauty of Robert's whole bag is that he has a good ear whether it be for the songs that he writes or other people's songs. He is getting a good song out there, one that people can understand. He's got very good diction so that you understand what he's talking about. He's able to convey the soul of each tune as he's singing and then complement with a guitar answer or a guitar solo in the same song. He's brilliant that way.

**"Even Flow"**
Pearl Jam
*Ten*
**JEFF:** The good thing that I find out of that type of music is the working of a band. Pearl Jam is a good example of each member of the band having to work together to create that form of energy, to create the whole song. Where the bass is complementing a certain chord phrase by the guitar player, the drums are complementing—and even showing the way of—the whole rhythmic changes, and so forth for the guitar and bass and the vocal and what the tune dictates. Of course, you have your little bit of improvisational solo breaks.

They play what are essentially old blues or jazz licks that are given loads of distortion with a wah pedal on them and people call it rock music. What is the Seattle sound? It's garage bands. They could have come from Seattle, Toronto, or London. It's that whole energetic, experimental [thing] as far as chords and rhythms, and then put a lyrical idea to it and vocals that match that whole thing. It's not necessarily anything new. If people are digging that and listening to that, it's probably a step in the right direction.

# GREG HOWE

**"For the One I Love"**
Robben Ford
*The Inside Story*
**GREG:** I think it's Robben Ford. The whole thing sounds perfect to me. I love that kind of groove, those kinds of changes. It's a little easier to sound interesting with bigger chords, major and minor 7ths, 9ths and 13ths, instead of major or minor chords. Plus, the chord progression is basic, so it's a little easier to sound interesting in terms of phrasing, playing over stuff like that. But he takes the fullest advantage of that, and for phrasing I can't think what I would have done that would have sounded any better. I love the tone. That's the kind of music I love to listen to.

Ultimately, what I'd like to be able to do is have phrasing like Carlton, Ford and another legendary guitarist who I heard for the first time recently, Joe Pass. That's what I would consider amazing. Joe Pass plays one perfect lick after another off the top of his head. It's instant and spontaneous. I'm nowhere near that. It's very easy to go nuts and play a million notes. But to be that clever and not have to work it out ahead of time is amazing. I want my second album to have a little more of those cool licks, clever phrasing and a little less of the unauthorized riffage.
**JOHN:** For a chops player, should I be surprised that you are a ZZ Top fan?

**GREG:** Those guys always play great blues. They do it with conviction. I like the singing, the guitar playing; the drums and the bass are super solid. Gibbons has the same element about his guitar playing as Albert Collins. There's so much conviction behind every lick, you can't help but believe it's there. You can't argue with it. He's got it. That's what I think a guitar player is. Anybody can play a blues lick, but it's not going to be done unless it's done for real. Those guys just do it for real.

# TONY IOMMI, GEEZER BUTLER
# (BLACK SABBATH)

**"Woodchopper's Ball"**
Ten Years After
*Undead*

**TONY:** I like that tune.

**GEEZER:** I'll have a pint. It's the sort of stuff we were doing when we first started off. Ten Years After were one of our heroes. Alvin Lee was billed as the fastest guitarist in Britain. One of our big breaks was when we did a gig with him. We supported Ten Years After and they really liked what we were doing, and Alvin Lee got us a gig at the Marquee in London. That sort of started the ball rolling for us.

**TONY:** We were doing that same sort of thing really. That's what we played.

**GEEZER:** All the stuff we had was all 12-bar blues when we first started. We used to do a lot of Willie Dixon stuff, and Howlin' Wolf and Lightin' Hopkins, Muddy Waters. Listen to the records, they were easy to play. So when we first came together, we had a gig in a week. We formed one day and had a gig a week later. We had never played together. So we learned eighteen 12-bar blues numbers in a week. It was great practice for learning how to play. It was mainly instrumental. We'd do a bit of vocal and then ten minutes of instrumental.

At that time there were hundreds of bands doing this. That was the way you had a band. You formed a band and you became a blues band and you jammed, and you formed into whatever music you were eventually known for. Today it seems like heavy metal replaced what the blues was then. Everybody gets up and does "Paranoid" and "Smoke on the Water" instead of the old blues stuff.

**TONY:** It was a great way of going into what we play now. You keep playing all the 12-bars and you start experimenting around those three chords.

**GEEZER:** Because it was so simple. Then you get bored of that so you go on to some other bit and you can feel yourself progressing all the time. Eventually you've got the background to go and write your own songs. Roots-wise, it's still blues-based.

**"Stockholm"**

Django Reinhardt

*Memorial*

**GEEZER:** Tony, it sounds like you messing about. Django is Tony's department.

**TONY:** I really like him. I like the way he fought through what happened to him with his hand and the way he mastered his own style of playing. He developed that technique that he could play chords with two fingers and the way he played them and some of the runs are incredibly fast. You'd never believe he only had a few fingers.

**JOHN:** Is there any style of music that you enjoy listening to or playing that would surprise your fans?

**GEEZER:** The Mothers of Invention. I used to love them. I loved Zappa's lyric approach. That influenced me lyrically definitely. As far as listening to, I listen to practically everything really except for dance music. I hate dance and techno stuff. I love playing funk bass. I've always loved playing that, but I would never record anything like that.

**TONY:** I play Frank Sinatra; I'm a fan.

**GEEZER:** He always comes up with these commercials, these daft commercials you hear on television. Then he will learn it on guitar. Coronation, Crossroads, all English (TV) commercials and soap opera things.

# ERIC JOHNSON

**"Django"**
John McLaughlin (with Jeff Beck)
*The Promise*
**ERIC:** Weather Report? [Jeff] Beck? Sounds like Beck on guitar. Is this on Guitar Shop? An older record? Is this a movie soundtrack? Is this Stevie and Beck? Don't tell me. Is that Cobham playing? Hammer on keyboards? I knew it was Jeff Beck. Sounds like Palladino on bass. McLaughlin.
**JOHN:** That's it, McLaughlin and Beck.
**ERIC:** Wow, I didn't know they played together. Is that Trilok Gurtu playing drums? He played great on that. Wow. That's McLaughlin. It sounds like it was probably cut with the Johnny Smith [guitar] with that new sound he's getting. McLaughlin sounds really cool. Which album is this, John?
**JOHN:** *The Promise* on Verve.
**ERIC:** What a signature. It's unbelievable. God, this is great. Beck is so original, his approach to playing guitar. I think originally that is a lot of what propelled me to try to learn more about guitars. I was kind of digging on doing all the Rolling Stones and Ventures and some of the Yardbirds stuff. I got into that. Then he came out with "Happenings Ten Years Time Ago," where it didn't even sound like a guitar, and "The Nazz Are Blue." I said, Is this a saxophone? It's amazing.

He pulls out of the guitar such an extraordinary sound. You are kind of transported at first glance to what the function of the guitar is. You think, Well, guitar does this. But he can show that it can do something much more. And I think, It's like since the advent of the '60s effect; obviously Eddie Van Halen made one of the biggest milestones since then. But I think one of the most unbelievable milestones since that original time is Beck's new technique with the vibrato bar. It's mesmerizing the way he can play melodies on the vibrato bar and his intonation is so good. It sounds like Bulgarian music sometimes. This was great, sounds awesome.

**"In the Wee Small Hours of the Morning"**
Wes Montgomery
*In the Wee Small Hours*
**ERIC:** This is tasty. This is Wes Montgomery. Wow, this must be off of one of the Rudy Van Gelder sessions.
**JOHN:** *In the Wee Small Hours* on Riverside
**ERIC:** Oh, it's on Riverside. This is great. I don't think I've heard this song before. I have—I'm not real familiar with it. Greatest tone a jazz guitarist ever got. I'm surprised it's on Riverside. It's got strings in it. I thought it would be later than the Riverside stuff. I guess it was that period just before he went to A&M and he started getting into the string thing.

To me there is no question, he had the most beautiful jazz guitar tone I've ever heard. I love Pat Metheny's tone; that is probably my next favorite tone. Because he is probably my next-to-favorite all-time jazz players besides Wes Montgomery. Wes had such an organic natural sound. I think he was real attuned to that. He used his thumb and that's a lot of what it was. But I think anybody that uses a pick can do just as well. It depends on how you use it and, obviously, the way he used his thumb. I think he was very conscious of the way his thumb hit the string, just like a violin player that uses a bow. You can have a $50,000 bow but it's got to be hit just perfectly to get the tone. I think Wes was real aware of that.

There's a book by Adrian Ingram and he's talking in that

book—there's quotes from Wes, and Wes is talking about his voice and his sound. The way he was talking about his music wasn't just my guitar playing or my licks, it was more than that. He was taking about his voice as a musician rather than his licks as a guitarist. I got that from him, really deeply, and also from Hendrix. I think Hendrix's approach was the same. He would be totally happy with the song where he didn't hardly play any lead, necessarily, but there is all this beautiful other articulation.

**"Flamenco Sketches"**
Miles Davis
*Kind of Blue*

**ERIC:** Is that John Coltrane? That's nice. This is Miles Davis from *Kind of Blue.* Listen to that tone. That's what lathers me up. Jeez, is that Bill Evans on piano? This is just sick. I just listened to this album recently. Man, that is really great. It doesn't get any better than this. It's just what kind of music moves you. If you are an artist, what is it that sonically or visually moves you? I don't know.

I feel like I'm in a precarious place because I love rock guitar and I want to peruse it and I want to keep the intensity and the tones and that whole thing, but there is something about it that is not working for me. I listen to something like this and I just prefer this sound. It's not a question of whether it's laid back or intense. It's a question of just the creation of the tone as it comes out. The tone that Evans is getting or the sax or whatever.

A lot of [my] last record, to be quite honest, I spent three years on the record and I spent a heck of a lot of that time sitting on the floor dinking with speakers and wires and tubes and cabinets and guitars to the point where it's like silly. I'm just trying to figure out a way to alchemize the parts of what I use to try to create for me what I feel is a better voice for rock guitar.

I want to stay in that idiom, but I want to personally improve my voice. It's a personal thing with me that I'm trying to do. I'm trying to figure out how I can improve my sound to where that distortion tone is a bit more pure and it's more of a voice that will interest me when I hear this track with the piano and the sax. or a violin player or a violist. That's just a personal thing. Everybody has different taste. This is just such a great record, just the sound. This will be a nice tape to play in my car. I like every song so far. God, that's just so good.

**"Spoonful"**
Cream
*Wheels of Fire*
**ERIC:** Oh yeah, this is "Spoonful" off of *Wheels of Fire*. I know this song lick for lick. That record was smooth. I wore the grooves off two copies. I don't mean that we all should have the same sound, but I don't know. You think about technology of equipment and the use of what the guitar is sometimes today in pop music. I don't get it. You listen to that sound. It just smokes everything. I'm stuck in that sound because it doesn't get any better.

I literally had this bible of records I carried with me everywhere I went. It included *John Mayall's Bluesbreakers, Super Session* with Mike Bloomfield, *Disraeli Gears, Wheels of Fire* and all three Hendrix records. Sometimes I would add other things to that, like Jeff Beck's *Truth*. But I would just carry those everywhere I went. I'd find a turntable, sit down and start learning all the licks.

## TOM KEIFER (CINDERELLA)

**"Move Over"**
Janis Joplin
*Pearl*
**TOM:** I've heard this a million times. You know what I like. Janis Joplin really inspired me singing. I love this song. It's those blues melodies. I love how the vocal goes with the guitar. That's what catches you immediately. The beat starts and that comes in and the guitar and the vocal are together. It has a great groove. Everyone said that band was a terrible band, but I disagree. They played together and they grooved. That's what matters.

**"Prison Blues"**
Jimmy Page
*Outrider*
**TOM:** I'd know that Sunburst Les Paul anywhere. Mr. Page. I like that album. They did this in one take. That's traditional British blues like Humble Pie and Led Zeppelin. I love that stuff. I like that song in particular; it kind of creeps along. "Prison Blues" has that low bass just walking. When I think of American blues I think more of the Delta blues and it boogies a little more.
**JOHN:** Tell me about your first brush with the blues.
**TOM:** One of the first blues artists I really got into was B.B. King. The kind of guitar playing that I was into was the blues style and this feeling thing. That's not something you can practice and learn.

It's something you get from listening to the record and jamming with other people. You can't sit down and just practice burning through blues scales. It's just not going to do you any good. It's a thing you really have to do. You have to play with other people, listen to it, be exposed to it. It's not as much a technical thing as a feeling thing. In that sense I wasn't doing scales for hours on end. I was more to myself in school than most people were because all I wanted to do was play guitar.

**JOHN:** Can you work on being more expressive on the instrument, or is it purely nature's gift?

**TOM:** You can get better. With blues you always hear something different in it. I thought I had a lot of licks down and I pulled out some Johnny Winter albums the other day that I had been listening to for years and I heard about 500 other riffs that I don't have down, and feeling and little pauses and hesitations I have to study. From one blues record you can learn for years. Every time you go back to that record and listen, you hear something different.

**JOHN:** Isn't that true of every record?

**TOM:** I'm sure it is. The thing I like about blues is for me it's expressive. That's the kind of music I feel good expressing myself with. There's no right or wrong; that's just what I feel good about. I'll go to my grave playing that music.

## ROBBY KRIEGER (THE DOORS)

**"Afro Blue"**
John Coltrane
*Live at Birdland*

**JOHN:** You guys played this entire song as part of the tune "Universal Mind."

**ROBBY:** Twice! There's a lot of melodies that we played. Mostly, Ray was a master of ripping off little melodies like that.

**JOHN:** I watched my bootleg tape of the Doors at the Hall of Fame and you played "My Favorite Things." You can't pawn it off on Ray!

**ROBBY:** That's right, that's true. Last night I not only did that, but I did "Summertime."

**JOHN:** The Doors had a lot of jazz in them.

**ROBBY:** Oh yeah. John Densmore played jazz before he played rock 'n' roll. He had a little jazz group that he played with in high school. We used to go and see all the jazz guys when they would come into town to Shelly's Manne-Hole in L.A. I used to see Roland Kirk, Miles, Coltrane, everybody. That was the greatest. At that time, I didn't hardly play guitar. I was just starting. I never thought I would be able to play any of that stuff. We used to idolize those guys.

**JOHN:** In the live version of "When the Music Is Over" you play a solo that has as much Coltrane in it as the Byrds' "Eight Miles High."

**ROBBY:** Yeah, I still do that. I play the songs where you can open them up and play. I use that solo. You can get pretty wild. On the real version of that, what happened was we just started recording solos and we had some really good pot that day. I think that's what happened. We recorded maybe five or six of them. We were trying to figure out which was the best one. So, we put this one up there and we really liked it. Somebody pushed the button by mistake and put two of them on at once and they just worked perfectly.

That song, we played it so much before we recorded it that we knew where we were going. In fact, the day we were supposed to record that, Jim had stayed up all night on acid. Of course, he woke me up in the middle of the night: "Robbie you've got to help us, man; we're dying. We're dying over here; you've got to save us." I came over about six in the morning and I took them out to Griffith Park. I thought maybe some nature might do them some good, instead of hanging out. We start walking out the door. I turned around and said, "Jim, you've got to put some pants on!" He didn't have nothing on. I dropped them in the park and then I go to the studio. I went, Oh my god, we're supposed to do "Music's Over" today. Jim is not here. How are we going to do it? Jim has got to be there on that piece because he kind of leads the whole thing, what comes next. Then again, we played it so much we sort of knew what he was going to do. So, we just put the track down without him being there. We kind of guessed where he would come in. He came in later, the next day or something and in one take did the whole thing perfect. He just followed it like we were all playing together.

**"So What"**
Alex Skolnick
*Guitar's Practicing Musicians Vol. 3*
**ROBBY:** That's good. Who is that?
**JOHN:** Alex Skolnick.
**ROBBY:** "So What"—I liked it, especially when they go into the

walking bass part. In fact, I'm going to do that tonight when we play this song.

**JOHN:** When it walked, it also went from organ to acoustic piano and the sound opened up.

**ROBBY:** Yeah. Good idea. On mine ["So What"] I use the guitar synthesizer, which is kind of cool. The problem with a guitar synthesizer is a lot of people don't realize it's a guitar playing. It sounds so much like other instruments a lot of times. I try to make sure that you know it's a guitar playing.

**JOHN:** You can mix in your guitar sound.

**ROBBY:** You can do that too. The other thing is you can play like a guitar. If you have a flute sound you can play stuff that you know a flute would never do, like slides or bends. It's kind of cool. I think that's the only song that I use just the synthesizer alone, no guitar at all. I use the Roland GR-50. To me that's the best one because it has sounds you can mess with a little bit. The newer ones you've just got what you get and it's harder to treat the sound.

**"Goodbye Pork Pie Hat"**

John McLaughlin

*My Goal's Beyond*

**ROBBY:** I don't know who that is. No idea. It almost sounds like Di Meola but Di Meola wouldn't use that few notes. I enjoyed it. It's nice music to have around the house, and I like the idea of just having the two guitars instead of the usual overproduced, overblown guitar approach. It takes some nerve to just do a thing like that, with just an acoustic guitar. I liked it.

**JOHN:** That was John McLaughlin doing "Goodbye Pork Pie Hat."

**ROBBY:** Oh, that's what that was. That's McLaughlin. Didn't Joni Mitchell do that one? It was good because he could get away with doing that because he's a good player. If some half-ass guy tried something like that, it wouldn't be good; it would be hard to listen to. It wouldn't make sense. But it kind of told the story.

# SONNY LANDRETH

**"Get Rhythm"**
Ry Cooder
*Get Rhythm*
**SONNY:** This always knocked me out. The first time I heard this, I was going down a highway in a van with John Hiatt. It was during the very early part of the Bring the Family tour. It was really cool because Ry had sent an advance tape to John to help him come up with a title for the album. It was great to get that sneak preview. The first thing to hit me about it was, Wow man, the sound.

For me, with this album, you can probably trace how Ry's sound has developed over the years. For me this is just the quintessential time for slide guitar, and I think he's it. That percolator rhythm and that funky finger picking technique on here is real infectious. I listen on different levels. There's the guitar thing and at the same time the tune and how they produced it. I really like the approach on this album. But his sound, he really went for it.
**JOHN:** I played it for you because you and Ry share this wonderful sense of bounce in your rhythm.
**SONNY:** The bounce, yeah. It's interesting that you said it because once I read an interview with David Lindley and he was comparing reggae, border music, Cajun music, calypso and the fact there is this element of bounce in all of them. I think it's a really good observation. I think in all these types of music a part of mas-

tering or getting close to that art form, is learning to feel that and being able to capture that when you play it. That's the thing. This is appropriately titled *Get Rhythm*. It's a real cool album.

**JOHN:** You have that bounce. You studied it or gone after it.

**SONNY:** That's from growing up in southwest Louisiana. With Cajun music you had the two step and waltz. To the outside ear it starts sounding alike. It's like anything when you get into it and study it. There's subtle nuances and getting what you call the bounce is a big factor. If you don't get that you don't get it at all. A lot of that has to do with the way they dance there. Music, dance, and food is all part of the thing there. I'm coming from both sides of the dance floor, being out on it—participating like that ever since I was a little kid—to playing in bands. I think it helped me.

**"No One to Run With"**

The Allman Brothers Band

*Where It All Begins*

**SONNY:** The first time I heard the Allmans was in Louisiana. By the time I heard Duane I was probably 19. I think it was 1970. The next time I heard them, without Duane at the Warehouse in New Orleans. Next time I heard them was without Berry Oakley. Watching all the changes they have been through, it still knocks me out when I think of a band being together for many years and how that translates to playing really live. They just stand out to me more than anybody.

There is something about when you live as comrades in arms, so to speak. You can know what everybody is thinking before it happens. You may change and do things onstage and you play in a way that you can't otherwise. You could put the greatest players in the world together but there is something about that bond when you get that close. Really, it is a kind of intimacy.

You can hear that on this track. They are playing live. That's like live to me. You can't duplicate that any other way. That's not just a matter of going and putting all the microphones up; it's a matter of being together for many years and going through the changes. My favorite classic twin guitar sound is that. Every time I hear it, it is one of the things that transports me back to those days when I first heard them and got into them so much.

I had heard about them from friends. They had been playing New Orleans and hanging out down there before they got known. I kept hearing about them. Finally I heard them and said, God, no kidding. One of the coolest things they did was their different approach to playing blues. And that progressed over the years. You start from the get-go on their first two albums. That's what really impressed me. Then you can start digging in and hearing their individual voices.

It reminds me of when the Band and *Big Pink* came out and blew everyone away because you hear three- or four-part harmony but there was an identity to each voice, instead of a more homogenized sound that most people go for. You can hear that in the Allmans and their playing.

Warren [Haynes], I have to say—talk about walking into some shoes to fill. I can kind of relate only in playing with Hiatt because of the Ry Cooder connection. The stigma of the legend is much more overshadowing when you talk about Duane Allman. Warren is great. I'm a big fan. He just fits like a glove.

They've got the sound. That's no small feat to be able to capture that. Whenever you look at a great band that had such an impact, they are one of the all-time greatest ever. When you see it go through the changes over the years, the first thing people look for is what's still left there. What can I still cling too? That's human nature. A lot of the great groups do their sort of reunion as a big thing this past summer and the summer before [Eagles, etc.]. These guys have been doing this as part of going through life's changes for them. I think that's a really beautiful thing. They have not only pursued it, they are still thriving.

**JOHN:** How would you describe their variation of the blues?

**SONNY:** They added voicings and they really zoomed in on the two-guitar role, whereas they very unselfishly could work around each other at the same time. It's a very symbiotic relationship to do that in a way that really ads to the songs. There's 12-bar progressions but they add a lot of colors. What always struck me too was such an identity with Gregg's voice and keyboards. I always zoomed in because I'm a [Hammond] B-3 nut. He would do little things and all of a sudden the song would shift and he would go to this organ and the tambourine comes out of nowhere. With Jaimoe, and all of them, I love the rhythm section because of the New Orleans influence.

**JOHN:** What about this song?

**SONNY:** It's a great song lyrically. It says a lot for someone who survived the journey and is thriving. The end of the song is so subtle with two minutes of Bo Diddley beat. Man, that's rhythm, that's what I love. You would think, Why did they continue? You've got to listen in the cracks to hear it evolve. You have to relax with it. I love stuff like that. When I heard incarnations of the band where it was mostly just Dickey, he blows me away. He keeps playing greater and greater. Everybody in the band, they all have their part in the group, and it is a really special thing.

**"Tell Everybody I Know"**

Keb' Mo'

*Keb' Mo'*

**SONNY:** I really dig the fingerpicking. It is always interesting to me taking cross cultural influences. When Taj was doing that, taking finger picking and adding different instruments that is kind of a direct line there from the Delta and the influences from those people from different countries are coming in from so long ago. That's Keb Mo. People I respect really rave about him. The greatest licks in the world are just that if it's not actually music in the way of making a song.

**"Sharp Dressed Man"**
ZZ Top
*Greatest Hits*
**SONNY:** That's really cool. I love it. I've always related to Billy [Gibbons]. I've noticed he likes these same voicings that I like to do, the chordal tuning. I hope I'm on the right track here—that hole in the root against the seventh and a wall of sound with the guitar. I don't know exactly what he is doing; it's a really big percussive sound too.

I remember the first time I heard one of his records and solos. I turned on the radio. It was midway through the solo and I picked up on some of the things he was doing. I thought, Wow, that's a soul mate there. I think he is a really tasty, real dynamic player. Obviously has spent a lot of time working on sound and phrasing. To me that's what it boils down to. He is a master. He popped in on a gig once in Houston. Tonally there is a real close thing. That's really exciting to me. I don't feel competitive. I get so excited about things like that when you see people on the same hive minding. There's something cool about that.

This band has a willingness to embrace the blues and be modern. They are not afraid of technology and to marry it with blues ideas. I think to really limit your options is really narrowing that dance. The way it's done, how it's used, it's got to be soulful. You've got to really feel something there. Who is to say whether it's right or wrong? They are open-minded to embrace the new ideas. There are people who I respect their abilities and what they do, but they say you're taking it too far from the source. Some people do that, I agree, and they get away from it, but certainly not in their case.

**"Sun Medley"**
Danny Gatton (with Delbert McClinton)
*Cruisin' Deuces*

**SONNY:** I never heard this. The first time I heard him I was playing with John Hiatt. It was at one of the NAMM shows. We played a club upstairs. He was just phenomenal. There's not enough words. He had all the technique you could ever want and then some. But he could infuse a kind of energy and genius in his playing. It grabbed anyone. It grabbed people who were not guitar freaks.

I was talking to the guys last night about it. It sort of transcends the ability he had. It was more the emotive aspect comes through his playing. A lot of guys are very technical and accomplish a lot in terms of method. I like when you have a combination of that kind of technique on that level, but the emotive aspect really stirs the soul. I always found it in his playing, in any of these off-the-wall recordings.

There was a French collection of a lot of different players from the U.S. It was originally entitled *Everybody Slides*. As it turns out, it had a lot of different slide players. There is one track with Danny on there. He would go from this kinetic thing and at the same time he hits his fingerboard pickup and there's this big beautiful round tone and real lyrical. He could do it all and all in one song. Danny's just is a master.

## ALEX LIFESON (RUSH)

**"Oh, Pretty Woman"**
John Mayall & the Bluesbreakers
*Crusade*
**ALEX:** We used to do this song a long time ago when we played in bars. This guy showed me "Snowy Wood" from the same album and I practiced that song for hours every day. That and "Spoonful" were easy songs to play along with. Of course, after that, Jimi Hendrix was just a step away.

Playing bluesy stuff is something I really love doing. When I sit around, play on my own, that's the kind of stuff I always play and I have always played. It's not a trendy thing. That's where I first learned the kind of stuff to play, from the second and third generation white blues players. But that's what I always learned to play. That's really the most emotional area to play from.

## STEVE LUKATHER (TOTO)

**"Crossroads"**
Cream
*Wheels of Fire*
**STEVE:** This is one of the best solos of all time. There is not one bend or wrong note in this solo. It's total state of the art, Eric Clapton at his best. It has everything: the phrasing, the build of the solo, the burn, the sound, the tone, the vibrato, the intonation, and the element of fun. It doesn't get any better unless it's "Voodoo Chile," which is state of the art in its own way. "Crossroads" is the ultimate and the fact that it's live makes it ever more the ultimate. You know it wasn't a punch in; it's Eric just burning.

I was hanging with Eddie Van Halen and this is one of his favorite songs. He plays it note for note. When I first heard it, it made me feel a certain way. I thought, This is incredible. I didn't realize the impact of it being live and what it was really all about until a few years later when I was getting into studying everybody's solos. Every guitar player knows the "Crossroads" solo, and if they don't, they should learn it.

# GEORGE LYNCH (DOKKEN)

**"Crosscut Saw"**
Albert King
*The Ultimate Collection*
**GEORGE:** The angry Indiana farmer. Oh man, there is something about this guy's playing that is so primal. He played the same notes over and over, but it just gets me on such a gut level. I don't know this song in particular. I was a big Albert King fan when I was young. I grew up on a lot of his music. I read somewhere that Hendrix learned from him. I figured if Hendrix learned from him, I had to go to the source and check him out. So I did.

He was my favorite player of that genre of blues players from that era. I never got into B.B. King. I always got off on Albert. He had this angry style. He was a big man. He had telephone cords for guitar strings and action way off the neck. It's all in his fingers. And at that time, I was listening to Hendrix, early Beck, and the first ZZ Top record. But the first ZZ Top record, to me, is a classic. When I was young I used to play "Brown Sugar" from that album. My copy band actually won a battle of the bands trophy with that song. I like listening to old blues like Buddy Guy.

I have never really done my homework with the blues players, like I should. That's like a lot of things in my life that I haven't really pursued fully. It's the same way with a lot of jazz players. I haven't done my homework. I don't really know people's songs; I don't know their records. I don't even know a lot of players by name. I just dabble in it. One thing I hope to do some day is to be able to go out and get a whole library and listen to it. To become a student of this type of music, which I should have done a long time ago. I don't know if it would make a difference in my playing, but sometimes I'm embarrassed when I talk to people about simple things that relate to guitar and I don't even know who these guys are. I'm probably most familiar with Albert King. Still, I couldn't name an Albert King record.

## TONY MACALPINE

**"Steppin' Out"**
John Mayall & the Bluesbreakers
*Blues Breakers with Eric Clapton*

**TONY:** It's really bluesy playing. The kind of blues I like is more on a Robben Ford vibe. This guy is a good player. I think I'd like more of a typical approach to blues. The licks that he's playing are very boxy sounding. It's not going outside of the pentatonic. I like a little bit more of the chromatic weaving. I didn't like the guitar sound. It wasn't that interesting because it was very predictable as to where he was going.

**JOHN:** That was Eric Clapton in the '60s.

**TONY:** It's an older record. If I heard it on the radio, I probably wouldn't listen to it. I was never a big fan of Eric Clapton. He never clicked with me. I really like Jeff Beck and Robben Ford.

# LONNIE MACK

**“Rock ’n’ Roll Doctor”**
Little Feat
*Hoy-Hoy!*
**LONNIE:** It’s sort of like something Hank Williams would have done with a horn section. It’s something I could have done myself at a time when I had the Cincinnati Kids band with the horns. It’s got a nice groove. Everything is spaced properly You can hear all the instruments. It’s junky. It’s kickin’. It’s not overdone. It’s happening in the right spots. I’m listening more to the music than the lyric. On a song like this, that’s what I think most people would do. It’s a feel song. As long as you said something that matches that kind of feel, anything would work.
**JOHN:** That was Little Feat.
**LONNIE:** I’ve heard Little Feat, but I didn’t put the song together with them. It’s music that you play in between the cracks. Ain’t no particular place you’re supposed to play. You can rest within the music sometimes when you’re trying to get a point across. Sometimes I’ll play ahead of the beat and then come back. Sometimes I’ll tell my drummer, Let’s play on top of it or right on it or behind it. Some songs need to have parts of that in all different places. There is a time and place for everything. The tempo of this song was right on it, in the pocket. The horns were probably playing a little bit above it, but that works. The rhythm section was right on it.

**"A Good Fool Is Hard to Find"**
Albert Collins
*Cold Snap*
**LONNIE:** To me, Albert represents what Chicago blues is all about right now. He does it well. He's got his own style, which is hard to find in straight-ahead blues. Everybody has copied the same licks from everybody so much, but he has a different approach to it. Albert usually plays right in the pocket.

Some of those organ licks sound like some of the old Jimmy McGriff stuff. Some of those licks were similar to a thing I have called "Chickin' Pickin'." The organ licks that I was listening to and trying to steal licks from were more like Groove Holmes and Brother Jack McDuff. I guess I'm a frustrated organ player. I never could play keyboards and that's probably why I like keyboards around me. I've got two keyboard players in the band.

This is the Chicago shuffle stuff. This is where a lot of those type songs were cut. Any organ player loves to play this kind of beat. I love it, too. It's a great jam feel. It's straight changes. You can't get lost, and anybody can play it. If anybody's getting together to jam and they ain't played together before, they are going to come up with a song and feel like this.

**"Every Hungry Woman"**
The Allman Brothers Band
*The Allman Brothers Band*
**LONNIE:** Too much is happening, and nobody is locking in with anybody. I just hear it as everybody jamming but nobody really listening to anybody else. The congas and the drums are not playing simple to groove and lock in anything. It's sort of free, with everybody in their own place. They have had a bad headphone mix. I don't like to say anything bad about nobody's music. I'd rather not say anything if I can't say something good. There was an organ punch that was really offbeat. It's really not together. The guitar solos sounded fine. The singing was fine. They should have

sent the band home and got another band.

**JOHN:** That was the Allman Brothers.

**LONNIE:** They didn't play on this one. It's too jumbled. I've heard lots of great things by the Allman Brothers. A lot of the guys playing with Gregg right now used to play with me. I love their music but this ain't one of the good ones. It's too all over the place.

**"Georgia on My Mind"**

Stanley Jordan

*Standards, Volume 1*

**LONNIE:** It's a Les Paul influence, that's for sure. That's some good guitar playing. The style is something between Django Reinhardt and Les Paul, with some classical Mexican bass lines blended in. I like it. I thought it was real good. It's obviously two parts. I've seen Stanley Jordan on the tube. Amazing stuff he can do all at once. I thought it was great. To be able to do all that at one time you've got to know more than I know.

**"Lowdown in Lodi"**

Freddie King

*Texas Cannonball*

**LONNIE:** I know a whole lot about this song because I loved ["Lodi"] by Creedence. As a shuffle it don't work for me. The first thing I hear is where the song is coming from rhythmically and I liked it the original way. It works as a straight beat. It makes more sense that way. I think you could reach out better on the song. It's a standard solo played around the melody line, which fits the song. You could have jammed out and got it too busy and made it even worse. The singing sounds like good blues singing, reaching out and going for it.

# YNGWIE MALMSTEEN

**"Jesus Just Left Chicago"**
ZZ Top
*The Six Pack*

**YNGWIE:** I love those guys. They are the boogie band. They have that down. They have a lot of soul. For some unexplained reason, they managed to work within a very limited area and not become boring. I play that stuff in my car all the time, which is probably why I've had so many wrecks. I particularly like this song. They have very witty lyrics. I don't know much about them, but they have the right chops. I don't think anybody could pull it off as well as they do.

This song gives a pretty good picture of what they're all about. Billy [Gibbons] does it right. He sounds good. I think that solo was played on a Strat. It was played really [well]. It's not quite as good a solo compared to his others, but it's all there.

# MICK MARS (MÖTLEY CRÜE)

**"Statesboro Blues"**
The Allman Brothers Band
*At Fillmore East*
**MICK:** "Statesboro Blues" was one of the first songs I learned how to play slide guitar with. The very first song, when I was 17 or 18 years old, was "Tell Mama" by Savoy Brown. I sat there with a lipstick tube for days figuring out how to play it, and "Statesboro Blues." And that's when I discovered the Allman Brothers, too, and that's when I started playing slide. But Duane Allman, to me, was the best slide player ever. I wanted so bad to capture his attitude, that tone. It sounds almost like a harmonica. I wanted to do that real bad, but I didn't [laughs].

**"Albert's Shuffle"**
Al Kooper (with Mike Bloomfield)
*Super Session*
**MICK:** [Mike] would always hit these notes in his licks which were in-between. He would bend it between. It would be between flat and sharp. I like Michael Bloomfield. He's, you know, that blues guy; I just like the way he played. It was tasty with a lot of feeling.

**“Big Bad Moon”**

Joe Satriani

*Flying in a Blue Dream*

**MICK:** Sounds like “On the Road Again,” Canned Heat. Who is it?

**JOHN:** Joe Satriani.

**MICK:** I’m surprised because he is playing some licks that I know, those blues licks. I can never say anything bad about Satriani because I think he is great. It’s cool. I’m glad he is not limiting himself. The blues is a lot simpler than all the other stuff he is doing.

## ERIC MARTIN (MR. BIG)

**"Respect"**
Otis Redding
*The Ultimate Otis Redding*
**ERIC:** Stax/Volt. It's Wilson [Pickett] or Otis [Redding]. It's "Respect," an Otis Redding song. This is the "Try a Little Tenderness" days that I am well aware of. I think Wilson Pickett emulates Otis and they copy each other. Otis is the man. I wouldn't say this song is my thing. It's an influence but it's not my thing. I'm a major Otis Redding, Wilson Picket, Stax/Volt kind of character. A Memphis soul kind of guy. I was a Motown guy when I was little kid. Stax/Volt was my transformation to manhood.
**JOHN:** What is your Otis song?
**ERIC:** "Mr. Pitiful," hands down. It's my "Star-Spangled Banner." "I've Been Loving You Too Long" was probably the best part of Monterey Pop. I love great singers, and the way Otis Redding touched me was like a light switch that turned on inside of me. When I was younger, I used to listen to a lot of Motown. To me Motown was great, but kind of first love, puppy love, masturbation love. Stax/Volt was sticking it in. On the song you played here, you can hear strains of Wilson too. That sounds like "Duck" Dunn, Steve Cropper, Booker T, Al Jackson, the guys in Booker T, the best fuckin' rhythm and bombs band, as I like to call it, in the world.
**JOHN:** What are the qualities of the great singers?

**ERIC:** First-of-all, great singers are in tune. You've got to be in tune. You can skate around it and be stylistic, but you've got to stick to the note. Also, you have to be a live singer. You can tell Otis and Wilson and Sam & Dave are from that genre.

It was tough for artists in general in the '60s, but it's probably more tough for a black artist. It was like, Okay kid, give it to me right now. You've got one chance to record it. Do it now. If you suck it's going to cost us a lot of dough. Just give me your talents. I'm not trying to be prejudiced. I'm trying to say they had one shot and they blew their full load. That's a great singer.

I'm by nature shy. People say to me, "You don't really articulate; you kind of spit it out." I do at times. These singers have touched me and turned me to stand with pride as a vocalist. Soul can give you swagger, attitude; it can be used almost like a shield. If you are a timid little mouse, this kind of musical shield is something you can stand behind.

## BRIAN MAY (QUEEN)

**"East-West"**
The Butterfield Blues Band
*East-West*

**BRIAN:** It may be Mike Bloomfield; I don't know. Whoever it is, I don't particularly like the way he's playing. It doesn't follow the chords and it seems like he doesn't quite know where he's going. I'm going to get shot for this, but it doesn't extract anything from the song structure that's underneath. It seemed like he was off on his own. I like the harmonica player very much. If it is Mike Bloomfield, I would qualify it by saying that I love some of his playing.

**JOHN:** It was Bloomfield from the *East-West* album.

**BRIAN:** I never liked that album. I was bitterly disappointed with it. I loved the previous one, *The Paul Butterfield Blues Band.* I played it inside out and backwards, until it wore out. I adore that album and hate *East-West.* I couldn't figure out what they had done. It seemed to suddenly lose its feeling and harmonic content.

# JOHN McLAUGHLIN

**"Lowdown Midnight Boogie"**
John Lee Hooker
*Southern Blues (Roots of Rock n' Roll Vol. 11)*
**JOHN:** He has great foot. As a guitarist it's hard to hear something like that after hearing Robert Johnson. Robert Johnson was such a wonderful guitar player and a monster singer. Unfortunately, I can't help but put them next to each other. This had a nice feeling, but the question is, what is he going to do with it? For feeling I can give it a good rating, but from a guitar point of view I can't give it too much. He's just happy and groovin' along.

## DAVE MURRAY (IRON MAIDEN)

**"Change It"**
Stevie Ray Vaughan and Double Trouble
*Soul to Soul*
**DAVE:** It had to be Stevie Ray Vaughan. You can tell straight away. When I heard his first album a few years ago, it was like he suddenly made me want to get back into the guitar. I've always loved the blues and listened to Buddy Guy and Albert Collins. I went to Antone's in Texas and Buddy Guy was at the front door playing on a 40-foot guitar lead. That sort of music is great in a club where it's smoky, people are drinking at tables. Stevie Ray Vaughan is an extension of the greats, a modern day blues player who still retained the complete feel of the blues guitarist. Vocally he is also right there.

I actually learned this song so I could go out and play it in the clubs. I haven't had a chance to play it yet because nobody else knows it. It's got the atmosphere. It's late night music.

With Stevie Ray Vaughan it's the way he plays, his feel and that he rings them notes out of the guitar. He attacks it. The way he holds two strings together is reminiscent of Hendrix. You can say more in one or two notes than you can in a million, and he actually does that. He is one of my favorite guitar players.

**"Theme for an Imaginary Western"**
Leslie West (with Jack Bruce)
*Theme*

**DAVE:** Great chord progression, lovely solo. The guitar sound is modern, heavy on the chorus, yet it's very subtle. It's very colorful as far as the flanging and chorus. It's not like the old Rockman or GK amps. You've got the studio effects put in there. I'm trying to think who the guitar player is. I loved the vocal. I loved the whole feel of the track. To carry a song at that tempo and still have you captivated at the end of it is great. A lot of songs that are one tempo start and don't go anywhere. This is one beautiful ballad.

**JOHN:** The vocal was Jack Bruce.

**DAVE:** I was sitting here thinking it sounds like Leslie West and I couldn't quite make the vocalist out. Then I figured it was Jack Bruce and maybe Leslie West. I thought that can't be. Actually it was "Theme for an Imaginary Western." I haven't heard that for about ten years. This is great. Is that on an album? I've got to get it. It is brilliant. The whole song has a lot there for guitar players. There is a lot of depth to that one. I loved the solo. It's gentle. On a song like that it's so easy to go flying into screaming guitar solos. It's a nice clean solo that complemented the song. It sat right in with the track.

He's a great guitar player. Jack Bruce was great vocally. It gets ten out of ten. It's better than the original. It's another planet really. It's easy to listen to. A song like that, which was recorded over 15 years ago, shows the songwriting is there. It doesn't sound dated at all. Some songs are recorded again and they sound a bit dated. That holds up even better than the original. It's brilliant. I'm going to go out and buy it.

## OZZY OSBOURNE

**"Billie's Blues"**
Billie Holiday
*The Definitive Collection*

**OZZY:** It's blues. I started playing blues years ago. I can appreciate it. It reminds me of sitting in a bar someplace. It's nothing I would go and buy because I'm a different person then; I was in this stage. When Sabbath first started, we started playing that kind of stuff in clubs and bars.

**JOHN:** Did you like it then?

**OZZY:** I like it now. I still like it a bit. She has got a great blues voice. She is obviously somebody. You are going to blow me away when you tell me. I can see that twinkle in your eye. It's someone like Ella Fitzgerald.

**JOHN:** Billie Holiday.

**OZZY:** I can appreciate it. It's not my cup of tea. It doesn't make me rush out and buy it.

**JOHN:** Could any blues voice do that?

**OZZY:** Not anymore, I don't think. I've gone a different way. I started playing blues. It's the easiest thing because it's only 12 bars. You can sing any old words to it. Everyone was the same thing except there was a bit of harmonica and then a guitar solo. I don't know if it happened over here but it was around the time Candid was happening in England. It was a big drive of early Fleetwood Mac and John Mayall. It was a big thing to go see John

Mayall's Bluesbreakers from that era. I suppose I owe my living to that era.

# JOE PERRY

**"I Hate Everybody"**
Johnny Winter
*Second Winter*
**JOE:** I think it's Mike Bloomfield, but I'm not sure. I thought it was real good, a classic Chicago kind of style. The guitar solo was real good. It's not James Cotton?
**JOHN:** It's Johnny Winter.
**JOE:** He's a wiz. I really like his playing, especially his slide work. In the early days when I started going to see the blues players, it was probably Johnny Winter because he was still doing it in kind of a rock format. I think rock 'n' roll is our folk music today. It is people getting together and listening and getting into a common thing. That's what folk music is. The real blues is sitting around your porch with friends and jamming.

## DAVID LEE ROTH (VAN HALEN)

**“Caldonia”**
B.B. King
*Now Appearing at Ole Miss*
**DAVE:** Straight whiskey in a paper cut. There’s a lot of smoke in the air and people dancin’ without takin’ their feet off the ground. Sexy fat ladies are squeezed into tight dresses, like they’re gonna burst when you get ’em behind closed doors. Feels like elephants walked across your tongue and they’re slowly working their way down into your stomach. The only way to get rid of it is to do it again the next night.

It’s not the most technically proficient guitar playing or production, but it’s got all the feeling that I started off with. That’s very important to me. It’s the essence of this kind of music. It’s not dirty, it’s not gritty; it’s like dirt under your fingernails with a tuxedo. It’s not ever saying the letter *S* when you speak English.

I think it’s one of the Kings, either B.B. or Albert. It has that distinct guitar sound and I know a lot of people have copied that. I don’t know if he does it on purpose or not, but it sounds like he fades in and out, like maybe he didn’t have enough sustain. Sounds like the brass have a real look of distain on their faces, elegant boredom. The vocal is gritty and he’s been drinkin’ said whiskey out of a paper cup. He’s singing the blues, but he’s obviously transcended it. They’re celebrating emotion and life, the good stuff and the bad. It comes full circle now. We celebrate tennis shoes just like we celebrate fancy leather shoes. This music is both. It falls neatly in between the two.

# DAVID SANBORN

**"Groovin' "**
Hank Crawford
*Heart and Soul: The Hank Crawford Anthology*
**DAVID:** Hank Crawford is my man. I don't know what this tune is. It is one of Hank's arrangements. He had such a great, elegant and clear way of orchestrating, especially for a small band. He did a lot of the charts for the old Ray Charles small band, when he had like five or six horns. David ["Fathead"] Newman did too. So, it's Hank and Fathead together. Those two guys were the two guys that inspired me to play the saxophone. Hank is immediately identifiable to me from the first tone. There is something about his tone and way of phrasing and attack and his way of sustaining notes that is just so memorable to me. It's so heartfelt and soulful. He's the guy who really cuts right through to the heart for me. There's very little in the way from his soul right to your heart, when you hear him play.

The first time I heard him was on the record *From the Heart*. I had at least four copies of the album and three copies of the CD. "Don't Cry Baby" is probably the tune that really did it for me. It's one of those really slow ballads that only Hank could do. Back in the '50s Ray went through a period where he would play tunes really slowly, like "Drown in My Own Tears." You could have lunch between the first and second beat. "Don't Cry Baby" was very much in that vein, if you pardon the expression.

**JOHN:** Did you try to imitate Hank Crawford?

**DAVID:** I don't think I would ever flatter myself to say that I sounded like Hank; I certainly tried to emulate him. Some of it was because there was simplicity and an emotional directness to his playing that got me right away. In the ensuing years my respect for him has only grown. I realized that simplicity has a real elegance and high level of musicianship. Very few people understand that one of the hardest things in the world to do is play a ballad, especially play a ballad as slowly and with arrangements that were as revealing as those that Hank would make.

On *From the Heart* there was no piano. It was just guitar played in the Freddie Green style, bass, drums, and lot of space. Hank could leave a lot of space and maintain tension. The thing that I have always appreciated about musicians is their understanding of the importance of space and silence. Sometimes music seems to be interpreting the space or interrupting the silence. I don't think I was ever as effective at using the space as Hank was. I think I used the space well on "Lotus Blossom" and "Imogene."

**"This Here"**

The Cannonball Adderley Quintet

*Cannonball in Japan*

**DAVID:** Cannonball and Nat, you can't get any tighter than that. It sounds like one instrument. Unbelievable. That's "This Here." No matter how much respect Cannonball gets, I still don't think he gets enough. When he came on the scene, he just blew everyone's mind. Forget about what a creative musician he was; on a purely technical level, he was one of the best saxophone players. He was so clean. His phrasing and execution were so clean. He had so much command over the instrument, it was scary.

There is one tune he does on an album called *Nippon Soul* called "Easy to Love." I think it's the first cut on the album. It opens up with him and Louis Hayes [drums], and they play so fast and he is so clean. You never get the sense that he is not in control of the situation. From the first time I heard him with Miles Davis to the albums he did with his brother [Nat]. I remember he got really maligned when he was doing this music, back when funk had a whole different meaning. Songs like "This Here" and "Work Song" were considered to be a sellout.

He was so personable and so into involving the audience. He was accessible and I don't know if many people know this, but Cannonball was a music teacher in Florida before he really came on the scene in New York. He was a music teacher and you really get that sense of him enlightening people. He has that kind of patience and ability to articulate ideas in a very clear way.

**JOHN:** Were Cannonball and Crawford the fathers of instrumental pop?

**DAVID:** No, I think you would have to go further back than that. Louis Jordan to a great extent was the father of rock 'n' roll, taken from a certain perspective. Listen to jump music that came out of boogie-woogie and some of the early players like Arnett Cobb, Red Prysock, players that came out of the big band swing era like Illinois Jacquet. His solo on the Lionel Hampton version of "Flying Home" was in a way one of the first rock 'n' roll saxophone solos. That was a great solo.

One of my great memories is *Life* magazine doing an updated recreation of the famous "Great Day in Harlem" shot. Instead of having 30 people they have like 300 people, or whatever it was. I was included. At one point somebody started just singing "Flying Home" and gradually more and more people joined in. When we got to the solo, people started singing the solo. There were like 300 people in unison singing this solo. Everybody knew it. It was a great moment to realize that all of us jazz musicians of all ages, we all knew that solo. It had such an impact on everybody. It was a great moment in music.

**"How Come U Don't Call Me Anymore?"**
Prince
*The Hits/The B-Sides*
(segueing into the same song by)
Joshua Redman
*Timeless Tales (For Changing Times)*

**DAVID:** Prince. Sounds like a demo. Is that Josh Redman? I didn't know he played with Prince. I didn't recognize it because of your segue. I love that record, I know that record. Josh is one of the great saxophone players. He has got that perfect combination of a lot of heart and a lot of brains. As good as he is now, he is only going to get better. His musicianship is only going to deepen and broaden with the years and he is already great now. He has got such control. He doesn't use his technique as an end in itself. He uses it in the service of the music. This is a good example of that. He is accessible without being condescending or cynical.

We played opposite each other in the south of France. He played some very difficult, challenging music, but he brought the audience with him. He opened the music up for the audience and brought them in. It wasn't forbidding. It was as if he was saying, Come on, you will enjoy this. I am just in awe of anybody that can do that. That can challenge people and make them really feel good. It's a difficult thing to do, especially in this day and age because people's attention spans tend to be much shorter. Josh is so good at that.

**JOHN:** What about Prince and this song?

**DAVID:** I like the raw quality of Prince's version. It almost sounds like a demo. The piano's got a little bit of an off thing to it. Just slightly out of tune. The intervals aren't quite ringing. It sounds like you are right there with him in the room. Those are my favorite records, the ones that are not perfect, that are not really polished and slick. I don't want to generalize, but nine times out of ten I like music that has more of a raw quality to it. I like music that puts you in the moment. To me those kinds of production values put you in the moment. You can hear somebody taking a breath in.

## CARLOS SANTANA

**"Double Whammy"**
Lonnie Mack (with Stevie Ray Vaughan)
*Strike Like Lightning*

**CARLOS:** They are both extremely special musicians. When I first came to San Francisco, Lonnie Mack was one of the first ones who was on the radio. For a long time, he's been really important to the guitar world, his contribution, his input and his vision. It's his attack, his execution, his choice of notes and phrasing.

I also use the same principle for everything. I always say when a dog has puppies, you always see a little puppy who separates himself from the rest. He finds a shoe and tears it apart. That's the same thing when you take a solo. One way or the other you've just got to tear it up. It's the same principle for John Coltrane or B.B. King. It doesn't matter how you do it, just tear it up and have a good time.

This is a great collaboration. I haven't heard the whole album but I'm looking forward to it. This sounds great. It sounds like they're just having a straight good time. I would like to hear it with big speakers, but it still sounds great.

**JOHN:** It was switchblade time.

**CARLOS:** That's what it is. Some people are not concerned with playing a million notes a minute; they are more concerned with touching every part of your body as much as possible. That's what they did.

**"I Got Some Help I Don't Need"**
B.B. King
*L.A. Midnight*
**CARLOS:** For my personal taste, he is number one. There's a lot of Kings that have contributed to the blues. B.B. King, Albert King, Freddie King, and my father-in-law, Saunders King. B.B. is tremendous. I heard the best of every player and B.B. is still the summit of feeling. No makeup, no flashy licks. He has them when he wants them. A lot of kids are impressed with flashy licks, but you can also reach the kids by sounding like B.B., with pure simplicity and feeling. B.B. is just the best at that.
**JOHN:** Were you born a stylist?
**CARLOS:** I was born with the gift of music. We are all born with different gifts. I knew I was going to be a musician and I didn't care about algebra or anything else in school. It was either a blessing or curse. I knew when I was in junior. high school and high school that nothing else would matter to me.

The last day of Mission High School in San Francisco people were saying, "Hey, what are you going to do tomorrow, man, when you are out of school?" I said I'm going to be playing with B.B. King and Michael Bloomfield. They started laughing at me. I said, "Why are you laughing?" They said, "Oh yeah, right." I said you can laugh all you want to, but that's what I'm going to do, man. I'm going to play with Michael Bloomfield and B.B. King and all these incredible people because that's what I want to do. That's who I am.

For me it was easier because my laser beam concentration once pointed wouldn't [let anything] deter me from hanging around Miles Davis or Jerry Garcia or Bill Graham. I just knew that that is what I wanted to be. Later on you learn about your notes and chords and Fender amps or Marshalls or Boogies or guitars; they are not so important as your principles or emotions. Those are really the tools.

**JOHN:** How can young players let their vision out and develop their voice?

**CARLOS:** Keep bending notes until it doesn't sound whiny or weird. Until it sounds like a voice. For example, learn to develop and crystallize your own fingerprints. In one note you can tell Eric Clapton from Jeff Beck. So, learn to go inside that note. A lot of musicians play over the note; they don't get inside the note. It's like a beer that has a lid; you can't get inside of it. Learn to open it up and go inside of it. Get wet with it. The first rule of music is if you feel it, people are going to feel it. If you don't feel it, why in the hell should they? That's the first rule of music. So, learn to feel.

I'll tell you a funny story. One time they asked Dizzy Gillespie, "How do you get that high note?" He was a pretty funky guy. He says, "You have to pucker up your asshole." You have to do certain things with your body and heart. Like I told you, soul, heart, mind, body and *cajones.* You have to connect all of those things so when you hit that note it's more than a Fender guitar or Ernie Ball string or a Marshall amp. Listen to Peter Green play "Supernatural"; it's more than a Fender amplifier and a Gibson guitar. That's what I'm talking about. That's what I want the kids to understand. Transcend the instrument. You are the instrument. You go inside and bring from within yourself that note that says, Wow, that is a new person.

**JOHN:** Can you recall the first time you pulled that out in yourself?

**CARLOS:** Yeah, in "Samba Pa Ti." It sounded very different from Michael Bloomfield or Peter Green or Eric Clapton. The first time I heard that I said, Ooh, that sounds like somebody really personal and dear to me. A lot of people claim when they heard "Samba Pa Ti," whether it's in Japan or Africa, that the song is really personal to them. Obviously I touched something deep in myself and when the people listen to it, it touches something deep inside themselves that they relate to.

# BLUES SARACENO (POISON)

**"Hustled Down in Texas"**
Johnny Winter
*Second Winter*
**BLUES:** Johnny is one of my favorite guitar players. This is kind of a cool tune. I've never heard him use a wah pedal before. I like the fact that it's raw, no reverb, no nothing. It's just straight. You could tell that it's one take. Johnny is my favorite guitarist because whenever you hear him play you know it's Johnny. Not only that, he's got this energy. He just plays and plays. The show will be over, the lights will be on, they will be sweeping the floor and Johnny is still onstage playing. He just never stops. He's got that real aggression when he plays. If he drops a note that note has been dropped and that's the bottom line. He doesn't care, he doesn't stop. He is relentless when he plays. That is the coolest thing. Plus, he's got a typical rock 'n' roll voice.

On this track he does all the typical Johnny things. He's like the kid in school you would punch and he wouldn't go down. He never stops. When everybody else plays, they'll do the same lick faster or slower. Johnny never plays the same lick twice. He has always got a new idea. His mind just takes off. His guitar playing tells a little story and he'll just go and go. He never seems to run out of ideas. It's the same blues type licks but it's always a new lick. And he always fits the tune.

**"Superstition"**
Stevie Ray Vaughan
*1990 radio broadcast*
**BLUES:** That's Stevie Ray. It's tough because he was the only guy who took a Strat and made it sound as fat as a Les Paul. The thing that was so cool about him, especially when he came out, is when he was playing the blues, which had been done a thousand times over, he gave it his own style.

I can tell him when he is playing on the Bowie album. You can always tell it's him. I don't know why it is, I don't know how he does it. He is a typical manly blues player. He has got the big strings tuned down. You know he uses really high action. You know there is no gain on the amp. You know it is all volume. You can hear every last thing.

I am a big fan of his early stuff. Even off of *The Sky is Crying*, the sound he gets on that one tune kills me. For a Strat, that hurts. He is the type of guy that makes you sit back and go, I've got to get one of them. I'm a big fan of the first couple of albums. It's real raw, the bare bones. That to me was just SRV and his guitar and the bass player and his drummer. That was what was coolest about it. This is hip. He is one guy who played the blues with such good technique. He really could play every note. He was so clean and so articulate and so fast. He would take his fast licks, some of the speed pickers favorites, and he would do it in a different way. It was equally as hard to do. But he would pull it off and pull it out of nowhere.

On the first couple of albums he had a couple tunes on there that are so fast to technically pick. But it's not the chainsaw picking tone. He got a true Stratocaster sound, only beefed up. I like this tune. I like this version. I like a lot of his live album. My absolute favorite take on this tune is the BBA [Beck, Bogert & Appice] version, the live one from Japan. It was looser than this SRV version, but I liked it a lot because it was real raw. Any time I went to see his shows I got the feeling I got my money's worth a couple of times over. What I wouldn't have given to bootleg half of them.

# KENNY WAYNE SHEPHERD

**"Blues Power"**
Albert King
*The Ultimate Collection*
**KENNY:** I got it on the first note. I don't think I need to hear this one; I know it inside and out. His playing is just immaculate on here, but the message is what really rings true in my life. The message is the simple fact that everybody can get the blues, no matter what age you are. I can't exactly remember the first time I heard it, but I remember my reaction. It was amazing. My dad put it in the cassette deck and he was like, "Check this out." It blew my mind, the whole speech and everything.

Albert was one of the first guys that I tried to emulate. My dad was a radio DJ and programmer. I grew up around a lot of really good music. I was raised on James Brown, B.B. King and all kinds of stuff. I guess I was absorbing it a lot more than anybody really knew. I am still taking licks from Albert King.

Listen to the dynamics in this song. When he's talking in the band, it's really low. When he comes back in, he plays that fiery guitar with the signature stops and the three-note bends. It's all Albert all over. He is another guy who couldn't read or write [music] that great. Everything that he learned he learned on his own.

I learned by listening to records. I don't read music. I have never taken any lessons. I play by ear and what I feel. I played along with [Albert's] *Live Wire Blues Power*, the Robert Johnson boxed set, Muddy Waters, anything by John Lee Hooker and Buddy Guy.

**"Somebody Done Changed the Lock on My Door"**
James Brown
*Messing with the Blues*

**KENNY:** I'm not sure who it is offhand. I can't tell who is singing. I can't even say I've heard this exact song. It's cool. The guy that's singing almost has a James Brown quality to his voice. It's a really good swing shuffle. There's a lot of passion in the vocal. Sounds like James Brown to me.

**JOHN:** It is!

**KENNY:** Oh man, I can't believe I haven't heard this song. Wow, that's killer. James Brown did a bunch of blues stuff like "Night Train." He definitely can do it. It's a surprise to me because I thought I'd heard every James Brown song there was, so you pulled one that I've never heard. That's pretty cool. This is a good vocal. Listen to the phrasing. You can tell he is into it. James is very good at projecting his feelings through his voice. You want just as much emotion in the vocal as there is in the guitar and all the rest of the music. I'm not 100 percent sure how that comes out the way it does. I know that when you play what feels right to you, it just does. It's a part of maturing. It comes with the actual act of playing for a long time and knowing exactly what to do and what not to do. It's knowing when to cut loose and play something that is flashy and knowing when to play something that is only one note.

**"Rock Me Baby"**
Johnny Winter
*A Rock n' Roll Collection*

**KENNY:** That's wild stuff. Whoever this is, got this lick from "Voodoo Chile." It's Johnny Winter and "Rock Me Baby." This is a wild arrangement of this song. Totally different from the B.B. King version I know. It sounds pretty rockin'. The main lick is a

"Voodoo Chile" thing.

I was always a big fan of Johnny Winter. I really dig his playing. He is a pretty good singer as well. He has got a really good edge to his playing. Probably because he came from a rock background first and then started doing blues. I can't say that I picked up a lot of Johnny Winter licks note for note but I had a lot of Johnny Winter albums that I went through. I got turned onto him through my dad, but also through Muddy Waters, because he played with Muddy Waters for a while. I enjoy Johnny Winter's work.

**"Come On in My Kitchen"**
Keb' Mo'
*Keb' Mo'*

**KENNY:** I can't tell exactly who this is; it sounds almost like Keb' Mo' doing Robert Johnson.

**JOHN:** You got him both right.

**KENNY:** I haven't even heard his album. That's pretty cool that I got that. It's a really good arrangement. He did a good job of putting the Delta sound together with a whole band, because Delta blues back then was just a guy and a guitar, and that was pretty much it. But he's got the whole band going and it's a really good arrangement. This works for me.

Keb' Mo' is a great vocalist. He's got a very aged quality about his voice. He sounds very mature. He can do the traditional thing really well. His slide playing is good. I'm not sure what makes a good one because I'm not really a great one. I'm working on it now. I feel like if he can do Muddy Waters style or Robert Johnson style, he's got to be really good.

**"Shuggie's Boogie"**
Shuggie Otis
*Shuggie's Boogie: Shuggie Otis Plays the Blues*

**KENNY:** Is the song all instrumental? I'm not sure who this is. It jams. It's got some good licks. It's really driving. It's got a good beat to it. I like how in the beginning he introduced the different people and did a little bit of their style. He sounds pretty cool. He's got a lot of styles down, like Hubert Sumlin, B.B. King. He's done his homework. Sounds good.

**"(If Loving You Is Wrong) I Don't Want to Be Right"**
Nathan Cavaleri
*Nathan*
**KENNY:** I can't tell you who it is. This kind of blues to me is all right, but kind of lays there for me. Maybe it's the production of the song. The real R&B styles of blues like this, all the minor chords and the way it's processed, I don't go too much for that. You can take traditional tunes and make it sound more contemporary without having to make it sound like this. Like what Keb' Mo' did.
**JOHN:** This is Nathan Cavaleri.
**KENNY:** This is Nathan Cavaleri? Pretty good for such a young kid. I can say that. It's just not my approach to the blues.

**"Talk To Me"**
Babyface (with Eric Clapton)
*The Day*
**KENNY:** Tony Rich? Who is this? It's licks here and there. I think that was cool. I think blues licks are probably the best tasteful licks to put in any song. They are in a pretty good context here. The licks fit. The singer is good. I think the tone of the guitar could have a little more bite to it, but the licks are fine.
**JOHN:** That was Babyface with Eric Clapton.
**KENNY:** I know Babyface. I can't believe I just said that about Eric Clapton's tone. I can tell it's both of them, now that I've been told that. It's cool. That both of them got together and did this is pretty cool. I think it's perfectly fine. Babyface is a very good producer, songwriter and arranger. He knows what fits.

**“Crossfire”**
Stevie Ray Vaughan
*In Step*
**KENNY:** This song speaks for itself. It’s amazing. I think on Stevie’s last album he was at the height of his career. It seemed like everything clicked. He totally knew everything he was going for. It was everything that he was trying to release through his playing and his songwriting. It all had come to a head. You can hear it well on this song. You can hear it well on every song on that album. Everything is amazing.

# ROBIN TROWER

**"Got to Be Some Changes Made"**
Albert King
*The Closing of the Fillmore East*
**ROBIN:** This is a live album? This is a much better band than when 1 saw him last. He's bad. I don't know this track. Obviously, I haven't heard this recording before. He's playing fantastic on this. When 1 saw him in 1981 I thought his band wasn't up to much. He's the best guitar player I've ever seen live, without a doubt. He is just unbelievable. So much soul, forget lt. Soul is the main thing that counts for me. Obviously, he was a great player. But I've never been interested in technical ability. I love guitar players that can't even play, just for their feel. But he was just the most expressive. He gets closer to the human inside than any other player, without a doubt. That was the first time I'd ever seen him live.

I've always been a big fan. Him and B.B. King have always been the biggest influences. He was unbelievably good, even though the band he was with was iffy. He still shone through that. You hear people try to imitate him today, but it isn't there when you hear the original. He's influenced everybody. Whether they know it or not everybody has been influenced by him.

Influence is one thing, copying is another. These are two separate issues. It's all a matter of your viewpoint. I never sat down and worked out anybody else's guitar playing because I've always believed you can only copy the technical thing they've done. You cannot copy the feeling behind why they played that. It's most important that you feel what you're doing. You can copy that stuff and it will still sound great. That's the thing—these are great lines in terms of melody and phrasing, but it's really the feeling behind him that made him what he was.

**"Life Without You"**
Stevie Ray Vaughan
*Soul to Soul*
**ROBIN:** He put the beat in funny places. It's pretty typical of what I feel about Stevie Ray Vaughan. He's a wonderful player, lovely touch and lovely tone. His material lets him down for me. I think that's what stopped him from getting where he could have. He's got to join up with some writers. Who am I to judge, but that is my personal opinion. His material let's him down a bit. You've got to come up with the stuff if you're going to go on making records. I don't know who wrote that; I'm guessing he did. It's a shame because material is the hardest thing about this business, coming up with songs. When it comes right down to it, you could be the greatest player in the world. If you haven't got the songs, then the records just don't happen. That's not a good example of what Stevie Ray Vaughan did anyway.

It's not fair for me to comment on him. I don't know a lot of names of his songs but there have been songs where I felt he was completely at home. One I particularly like is "Cold Shot." That had something, that track. He got something going on that one. I don't want people to think about me, Who does he think he is talking about SRV stuff like that? I've been around a long time. After a while you get a bit of wisdom about these things. Obviously, I've been around awhile.

I think it's great that Stevie Ray Vaughan was successful. I like that because the kind of thing he tried to do, we need more people trying to do lt. Whether I really got off on him or not is neither here nor there; that's what 1 would like you to put into the article. What he was trying to do was very important.

## JAMES BLOOD ULMER

**"Fishin' Blues"**
Taj Mahal
*Taj's Blues*
**JAMES:** That's funny. The only thing make me relate to that is the guitar. I was trying to find out whether he actually tried to play the music from what he was singing. He didn't play the music from what he's singing. But he did play the guitar right with his voice. He made a unison with the voice and the guitar. I never really did that before. Not on a record. I did that by myself, when I was singing and I didn't care. I might do something like that, but not in public.

It's not harmolodic. The movement, the guitar sounds harmolodic. He's playing in a tuning that can do more for the guitar than for his voice. The sounds he was playing on the guitar, he could take those sounds and do more on the guitar than he could do with his voice. I hope he catch that big fish.
**JOHN:** That was Taj Mahal.
**JAMES:** Taj? I never heard him before. If it was trying to get someone's attention and get them interested in what he was doing, it's great. He's talking about some stuff that everybody can relate too. But he didn't play the music to the sound. He played the music for his voice. Singing and music is different.

# STEVE VAI (FRANK ZAPPA, ALCATRAZZ, DAVID LEE ROTH, WHITESNAKE)

**"Have You Heard"**
John Mayall & the Bluesbreakers
*Blues Breakers with Eric Clapton*

**STEVE:** That guy had some serious blues happening in his life. It sounds like somebody took his house, his car, his wife and his dog. One of the reasons I like things like this is because I can't play it at all. That style of blues takes a real attitude to play. It goes to show you that technique is just a device. It really doesn't matter what your technique is like. You can get your point across without, if you've got the right attitude and you don't worry about your technique. That song had some serious attitude to it. It sounded like what he was playing he was really into. I wouldn't want to meet that guy right after that take. I'm not a big blues fan. I probably lost a lot of fans by saying that, but the old I IV V progression never really kicked in with me. Unless, of course, it's done with conviction, as this was.

**JOHN:** That was Eric Clapton

**STEVE:** You're kidding. That's the first time I've ever heard Eric Clapton really play. I always listened to Jimmy Page and Jimi Hendrix. For some reason, Eric Clapton's music never made its way to me. I had *Wheels of Fire*, but I never knew that was him from that. I'm impressed.

# JIMMY VAUGHAN
# (THE FABULOUS THUNDERBIRDS)

**"Born in Chicago"**
The Paul Butterfield Blues Band
*The Paul Butterfield Blues Band*
**JIMMY:** Back in the '60s it was Paul Butterfield and all the guys. When I was 15, I used to have a transistor radio and I would put it on my guitar pickup and make it come through my Fender amp so it would be loud. That's what I think of when I think of Paul Butterfield. Plus, all the great guitar work. I dug the whole thing in general with those guys. I dug that kind of music. I like the guitar, the drumming, the bass, the harmonica. I was really kind of a blues snob. I was into Muddy Waters, the kind of stuff Butterfield got it from. I prefer that, but I like this stuff too. They were some of the first white guys I remember doing that. It sort of meant it was okay for me to do it.

**"One Mint Julep"**
Kenny Burrell
*Bluesin' Around*
**JIMMY:** Is that Jack McDuff? I used to get every one of those organ trio records that I could get. Right now I'm in the process of trying to find them again. I got all that Blue Note stuff again when it came back out. This was definitely one of the biggest influences

on my playing. I've even gone as far as getting a Leslie cabinet and playing on records with a Leslie, trying to sound like an organ.

What can you say about Kenny Burrell? He was always my favorite jazz guitarist, right from the first time I heard him. He was so bluesy. I love the blues. There's a lot of fantastic jazz players, but he is my absolute favorite. It's his tone and his phrasing and everything about him. He is completely free to do whatever he wants to do. I would like to be able to play what I hear like he does. I think he can play everything he hears as he's hearing it. They call it jazz and blues and this and that, but it's all the same thing; it's music.

**"Wham!"**
Lonnie Mack
*The Wham of That Memphis Man*
**JIMMY:** Wow, Lonnie Mack. I remember when I was a kid and that came out, I bought that record and brought it home. That was a 45 that I used to play on 33 over and over, trying to figure out exactly what he was doing. It was strange because he had a lot of hits around Dallas, but I don't remember him ever playing around here, so I never got to see him. The only thing I ever saw was the picture of him on the album cover of *The Wham.*

I loved his tone and his wild-ass guitar, but at the same time he was blues and he was my hero. "Chickin' Pickin'," "Susie Q," "Memphis," of course. If you didn't know how to play "Memphis" in Dallas, you weren't a guitar player. Nobody could play like him. They could play the notes and learn the licks and play the song, but nobody sounds like Lonnie Mack except Lonnie Mack. He used a Magnatone. It took several years before I figured that out. It was like it was from outer space.

I felt exactly the same way about Lonnie Mack when I first heard "Wham!" as I did when I heard "Purple Haze" for the first time. Just what in the hell is that? It's so far out, the neatest thing you ever heard. You don't even know what it is. Plus, it was called "Wham!" Whoever named that knew what they were talking about.

I can't say enough about Lonnie Mack. It sounds better than the guitar playing that's out now, when we're talking about what's popular on the radio. It had soul. I'm not saying that nobody has soul on the radio today because that would be crazy. When that record came out, the stuff that I liked had to have feeling. It had to be wild and it had to have tone on the guitar.

Nowadays you don't hardly hear that. Robert Cray is doing it. Los Lobos is doing it. But the kind of records that are usually on the radio are all keyboard stuff and MIDI stuff. I probably sound like a dinosaur sitting here talking about it, but I just don't enjoy all of that. I like some of it. I thought the Peter Gabriel *So* album was good. He was like a soul band from outer space. But it was somebody who had definitely been to Earth.

**"You've Been in Love Too Long"**
Bonnie Raitt
*Takin' My Time*
**JIMMY:** That's one of my favorite songs by Bonnie. I love that kind of Memphis soul guitar. It sounds like of like the stuff we did on *Tuff Enuff*, the same kind of guitar playing. I like it 'cause it sounds like a guitar. John Hall's got a good touch, the black rhythm in there and a great tone and feeling. I love it. I saw him on TV with her a few years back. I like Bonnie Raitt; I can't think of anything she's done that I don't like. With some artists, it gets to where you just like the way they sound, and it doesn't matter what they do. I'm that way about her.

**"Since I've Been Loving You"**
Led Zeppelin
*Led Zeppelin III*
**JIMMY:** Is this Fleetwood Mac? Is it Led Zeppelin? It sounds like somebody who doesn't know what kind of music they're trying to

play. I like Led Zeppelin, some of their stuff. I don't like this. It sounds confused. It's everything I hate all at once. I think Page is a great guitar player. It's not fair to talk about somebody else's music. It's their music, so what do I know about it? Personally, it just sounds like one day they decided they wanted to play the blues and they couldn't. It's lack of direction and too notey. It's whatever flips your switch. If it sounds good to you, then it must be good. That's the way I look at it.

**"Railroad Steel"**
The Georgia Satellites
*Georgia Satellites*
**JIMMY:** That's the Satellites. I like them. But that's not the way I would do it. I don't like that kind of guitar tone. It's too Les Paul-y and distorted for me. I use that sound too sometimes, but not like that. I prefer not such a rough tone. I like an ice pick sound that can hum, as opposed to a comb and a piece of paper over it.

**"Bring It On Home to Me"**
Van Morrison
*It's Too Late to Stop Now*
**JIMMY:** I dig Van Morrison. I always did. I like the guitar playing. I don't know who it is. I like Van Morrison because to me, he sings what he feels, and he don't care what anybody else thinks. He wants to please the audience, but in order to please the audience you have to please yourself first, and they have to see it or hear it before they're going to get it. Because if you don't like what you're doing, how do you expect them to? I like him because he's on his own trip. This was great live. He was doing this gig and having a good time. I wasn't there, but that's what I think.

**“Amazing Grace”**
Steve Vai
*Dudes (Original Motion Picture Soundtrack)*
**JIMMY:** I enjoyed that. “Amazing Grace” is one of my favorite songs. It’s a song I used to play for my dad. But I never played it like that. I think it would have been better without that chorus. I like the thing where he sounds like he’s got the bar wanged up and he lets go of it and comes back down to a chord. That’s the kind of thing I like, where you first hear it and don’t know what it is. You’ve wonder, What was that? That was fun to me. He’s good. I love the song. But tell the guy there’s another verse.
**JOHN:** What is the roll of the guitar in blues music?
**JIMMY:** Is there any other role [laughs]? I don’t think I’ve heard a blues record without a guitar on it. There may be some. Its role is everything. And when you play you have to think about it: Am I actually trying to say something or am I just playing a bunch of licks?

A lot of guys sound like they are practicing. I remember when I first got going, I spent most of my time copying B.B. King, Otis Rush, Buddy Guy and Magic Sam. Then one night I remember thinking, I was actually getting pretty good at copying and imitating the notes. I realized, I didn’t think this up so I’m wasting my time. What do I want to say? So sometimes I would just stand there and wail till something came to me. Because I decided if I do something that’s fake, the audience is going to know it, so I’d better at least be truthful.

# STEVIE RAY VAUGHAN

**"Blues for T.J."**
Larry Carlton (with B.B. King)
*Friends*
**STEVIE:** Tough enough. I like the way the arrangement's done. I like the way somebody has been listening to B.B. King strong. They've been listening a lot. Personally, I would bring the horn up a little bit and fatten the bass. Other than that, it's cool. These are people who care about what they play. They have completely different styles. One is more traditional and the other is a newer style. I'm wondering if it was someone else who had listened to a lot of B.B. I love B.B. These guys are really listening to each other.

**"Stormy Monday"**
The Allman Brothers Band
*At Fillmore East*
**STEVIE:** I've heard this before. Of course, this is a great band. It's hard to do what has been done in the jam session, which is to go ahead and get somewhere with three solos going on. Everybody has to pay attention to getting there quickly. I like their approaches. Everybody is playing their own style and not trying to outdo each other. I like going to the swing time in the organ solo. That's tough. I still like this. The Allman Brothers were good at knowing those times when strict choruses don't apply. If something starts feeling good, it's time to stay on that something. It's something

that a lot of zydeco bands and jazz organ players do. They get on a riff that repeats itself. Jazz organ players often find one note to hold onto while they play the rest of it. The point is, if that note stays good to you, stay with it.

**"Marching Out"**
Yngwie Malmsteen
*Marching Out*
**STEVIE:** He's obviously an incredible technical player. It's a different cup of tea than I would normally listen to and it's obviously done well. It does have a lot of emotion, but it doesn't have the same kind of impact or soul as the other songs I've heard. Listen to Buddy Guy. That would tell you more than anything I could say.
**JOHN:** Were records your first introduction to the blues?
**STEVIE:** That and my brothers playing made a big impression. I got to meet a lot of people who were blues players, not too far from when I started playing. I would hang out on Hall Street in Dallas. I saw a lot of bands play.
**JOHN:** Since you learned a lot from your brothers' record collection, and a record is a record, could you have grown up in New York City with those same records and still have developed the same?
**STEVIE:** Probably not, but the differences would mainly be things I wouldn't notice unless I left for a long time. It's the feeling of the people. I'm sure the heat has something to do with it. It's just a way of life around here.
**JOHN:** What characteristics does Texas blues have that make it different than the British blues of the late '60s?
**STEVIE:** There's quite a bit of difference, in different ways. Texas blues has more horns; it's a bit more uptown in style. It's also a little rougher-sounding and meaner. It's not quite so slick. Not to sound out of line, but the English people were copying Texas music, so it's gonna sound a little bit different. There's a difference doing it growing up in the surroundings that created it instead of

seeing it from a distance.

**JOHN:** I started off playing rock and went back to the blues. Did you experience anything like that?

**STEVIE:** I pretty much had all of my influences at the same time. It got heavier handed on the side of the blues at a couple of different places. I was pretty heavy into it early on and more so latter. In the middle there was more Clapton and Hendrix. But keep in mind that at the same time I was still listening to the original songs that the English blues people were copying. I was getting a good view of it because I was seeing it from both sides at the same time.

I was listening to Beck, Page and Clapton along with T-Bone Walker, Buddy Guy, Howlin' Wolf, Albert Collins and some Lonnie Mack kind of things. In fact, Lonnie Mack's "Wham!" on Fraternity Records was the first record I ever bought. I did my best to learn it. It's a pretty strong thing, a pretty tricky one.

**JOHN:** Like "Scuttle Buttin' "?

**STEVIE:** They didn't get it on the record jacket for the first pressing of the album, but that song is dedicated to Lonnie Mack. It's pretty much taken off his style.

# JOE WALSH (JAMES GANG, EAGLES)

**"Crosscut Saw"**
Albert King
*The Ultimate Collection*
**JOE:** That's Albert King. It's usual Albert King. I liked it. I really love Albert. He's got great string pulls and he's a wonderful guy. He uses his thumb and never uses a pick—which I always thought was very cool.
**JOHN:** It reminded me of your economical style.
**JOE:** I listened to him an awful lot. He had a lot to do with that.

# LESLIE WEST (MOUNTAIN)

**"Forever Man"**
Eric Clapton
*Behind the Sun*
**LESLIE:** Eric is my hero and I love this lick. It's typical of Eric, but for some reason he just jumps in the middle with the solo. I'm used to Eric playing the holes. Eric's solo is great, very Albert King. But it did seem like this was Eric Clapton, and you've got to have a guitar solo. The ride out uses a different tone, more of the woman tone. The most important thing to me in the beginning, after I figured out you could play more than three chords on the guitar, was the tone on the guitar. It doesn't really matter to me how fast the guy plays or how much stuff he knows, but what it sounds like.

**"Boot Hill"**
Johnny Winter
*Guitar Slinger*
**LESLIE:** Is this live? Is this Chuck Berry? Whoever it is, it's out of tune. He played the blues like Eric. I always relate back to Eric. Remember the wah he used on "White Room"? The reason he never used it after that was because Jimi Hendrix said it all with the wah. Jimi played blues the way this guy is trying to. It's Johnny Winter. He's very sloppy, but he's fast, faster than I've ever been. He misses a lot of notes. That's why I asked if this was live.

Sometimes onstage, you're not in perfect tune.

I never liked this kind of blues. This is not as good as his earlier records and it's the same stuff. He used to play with a better tone. It would be very hard for Johnny Winter to do something updated. When he started, there was a look about him and a lot of hype. It's hard to live up to that stuff.

**JOHN:** Did you find the more you practice, the better you get at knowing what and when not to play?

**LESLIE:** I went to see this jam at the Cafe Au Go Go in Greenwich Village. This is in the '60s. The Cafe Au Go Go was a place in the Village where you could go and jam. So they all got up and whammed around the progression. It was B.B. King, Jimi Hendrix, Paul Butterfield, Elvin Bishop [Al Kooper, Buzz Feiten], all these guys.

Each one of these guys got up and played a regular 12-bar progression. Elvin Bishop played everything he knew in the progression. Then Jimi Hendrix hooked up all his pedals and did everything he knew. The last guy to come up was B.B. King. He hit one note. He sustained the note during the whole progression. They were staring at him like they forgot what he knew. After I saw that, I realized that less was more. I call it urinating on the neck when somebody is playing so many notes; there's not a downbeat to be had.

# JOHNNY WINTER

**"The Very Thing That Makes You Rich (Makes Me Poor)"**
Ry Cooder
*Bop Till You Drop*
**JOHNNY:** I like it a lot. The vocal group is nice, but a little slick. It's real good fingerpicking style guitar and reminds me of Ry Cooder or Little Feat.
**JOHN:** It is Ry Cooder.
**JOHNNY:** It sounded a lot like Ry, but I thought it probably wasn't because he does more chords than actual lead playing. I don't think that was him singing. That's the most sure of himself I've ever heard him sing. I like this one. I have to get this record.

**"North Carolina"**
Robben Ford
*The Inside Story*
**JOHNNY:** I like it, but it's a little too clean for my taste. Everybody is laying back nicely and I guess I would like to have it a little more vicious. I'd like them to let it all hang out a bit more. The guitar player and the harp player were both real nice. I like to hear everybody go crazy. The voice sounds real similar to mine. It's done well but put together a little too neat for me.
**JOHN:** That was Robben Ford.
**JOHNNY:** He's a California guy? I've heard real good things about him. He used to be the Charles Ford Blues Band. That's

where I heard of him. I'd like to see them go crazier, but they've got their playing down.

**"Cruise On Out"**

Rory Gallagher

*Photo-Finish*

**JOHNNY:** That one definitely had what I was talking about. Everybody was just truckin' on ahead. There was no one being laid back. I like that one. I recognized a few Johnny Winter licks in there and some C&W. I have no idea who it is.

**JOHN:** That was Rory Gallagher.

**JOHNNY:** Oh, great. I'm glad that was him. I've always kind of thought we were similar. A lot of people have told me that. I kind of feel bad that I haven't heard that much of his stuff. I like the hell out of it, though. It's kind of sloppy. He doesn't worry about everything being quite so neat or in the perfect place. He just gets the message across real well.

**"Limehouse Blues"**

Chet Atkins and Les Paul

*Guitar Monsters*

**JOHNNY:** In the late '60s, everybody was asking how I compare myself to so-and-so. I don't really like to do those kinds of things, but I remember seeing in one interview that I thought I was just about the best at what I did. But I didn't consider myself a guitar player when I compared myself to Chet Atkins, Les Paul, Segovia, and players like that. These people grew up doing nothing but playing the guitar. They can do amazing things, and that's a perfect example of just great all-around guitar work.

If they were gonna sit down and play a straight blues or rock 'n' roll song, I know I could do it better. But this was just amazing guitar playing. If I sat down and played for the rest of my life, I don't know if I could ever be that good. I was sure that was Les Paul. I wasn't sure if the acoustic guitar was Chet Atkins. But they are two of the most amazing guitar players alive.

**"I Can't Quit You Baby"**
Led Zeppelin
*Led Zeppelin*
**JOHNNY:** I could get myself in trouble on this one. I remember that real well from the time I—quote—"made it." Robert Plant I knew before I knew this record. I love those guys. But for doing straight blues, they were one of the groups where I'd sit down and think, If people think that's real blues, they ought to hear me play. That was their first record, and they were trying to do a lot more copying of what blues people were doing in America. Now that they're doing their own thing, I like them a lot better. I never did like that album, and I certainly like them a lot better now.
**JOHN:** If I wanted to start a blues library, which records would be essential?
**JOHNNY:** Definitely both volumes of Robert Johnson!
**JOHN:** Why?
**JOHNNY:** Because he's that much better. You should have the *Best of Muddy Waters,* Sonny Boy Williamson, and Little Walter, on Chess records. To me, they really contain the best. Albert King's *Born Under a Bad Sign* on Stax is a great album. B.B. had one of the first blues records that was on the market in album form. I bought 45s from everybody. B.B. had a record called *Singin' the Blues* on RPM records. I got wiped out by it, it was so good.
**JOHN:** What's the state of the blues today?
**JOHNNY:** People think there's no blues left. The blues is not dead; talk to the people who are doing it. Blues people have to care. B.B., Muddy and Bobby Bland, they might have a nicer suite, and might get one extra meal, but they're doing the same thing. They don't have that much better a gig than the group. B.B King is big shit now, but when he started working, he worked his black ass off. That's what all of us have to do. I did all those same things, working 350 nights a year, driving hundreds of miles from gig to

gig. I've had my own private plane, but now I'm back to riding buses. I don't mind at all. I care a lot about what I do; I don't care about the money.

**JOHN:** What about someone like Mike Bloomfield?

**JOHNNY:** I have so much respect for Michael. He was willing to try and put that stuff across when nobody really wanted to hear it. You may be able to think of a million better players, but it's hard to think of many who did it before him. Michael really cared. He wanted people to know where he got his music from. He wanted to turn people on to the old people. There's no way you can compute what he did for blues, black and white. He started in the early '60s and he's still doing it. Him and B.B. King helped me out more than anybody in the world.

Michael had this club called the Fickle Pickle, where he would get people who hadn't had a chance to play. He would pay them $25 a night, which was $25 a night more than they were used to getting. It was incredible because Mike's parents were real rich, and he didn't take any money from them. He did everything on his own. He helped me out a long time before I ever made it.

When I first left Texas, I went to Chicago doing my club thing. I had a Silvertone guitar with strings that had been on it maybe five years. It was the first time I ever played with real blues people. I played guitar and Mike flipped out, grabbed the mike and said, "This is the greatest blues guitar player in the world." He didn't even know who I was.

I had to leave Chicago because I was starving to death. I went back five years later and saw him at the Fillmore. He still didn't know my name, but he remembered what he had said. Mike, B.B. and all these people, I thought they would have written me off, thinking, since he's getting big he doesn't need our help anymore. It wasn't like that at all. It's a thing I can't repay. They've already got it down. They don't want it to be repaid to them. I think what they want is to have it repaid to other blues musicians that are just starting out.

# ZAKK WYLDE
# (OZZY OSBOURNE, BLACK LABEL SOCIETY)

**"Illustrated Man"**
Johnny Winter
*Let Me In*
**ZAKK:** Very good Johnny. That rocks, man. That's killing. You can tell Frank Marino must have dug Johnny Winter too. I saw Johnny Winter play at the Benson & Hedges Blues Festival. I went down there to see Gregg Allman who was playing with B.B. King. Johnny came out and was killing, man. And all he was using were two Fender amps and a little Stereo Chorus pedal. This song is very good Johnny. It's killing. He just rips. He hasn't changed or compromised over the years to sell more records. He digs what he does and that's it.

## ANGUS YOUNG, BRIAN JONES (AC/DC)

**"Oh Well"**
Peter Green/Fleetwood Mac
*Jumping at Shadows: The Blues Years*
**ANGUS:** I know who it is, Peter Green and Fleetwood Mac. It's an old classic. I always liked it, even the studio one, though the one we heard is live. I think the original track of this got ripped off a lot. A lot of people have a great love for this band and many took a leaf out of this book. When I was young I went out and bought that record, just for this track. It was an inspiration. This track you can sit down and listen to and still like it more for the lyric thing and the way the guy sang it.
**BRIAN:** I love all that kind of stuff. The singer is singing it the way the band is playing it and it's a great riff. You could release this song today as brand new.

**"Boom Boom (Out Go the Lights)"**
Pat Travers
*Live! Go for What You Know*
**ANGUS:** It sounded like somebody trying to clone the old blues. The drums, singing and rhythm sound very American. Was it Van Halen?
**BRIAN:** It sounded for a moment like Peter Wolf. If you ask me for a straight opinion, most good little bands in the world could play that at any Saturday night gig.

**ANGUS:** It's one of those common live songs and sounded like a blow. The guitar was more based on technique, like, how many licks can I get in? He played all the blues licks in one box.
**BRIAN:** I've heard this a million times; not this song, but I've heard this all before.

**"Jitterbug Waltz"**
Arthur Blythe
*In the Tradition*
**ANGUS:** I prefer old Dixieland swing to this. I love Louis Armstrong in some of his early records. I like all that Basin Street sound. It's all up music. That Dixieland is the most danceable music in the world to me. I can bop till I drop.
**BRIAN:** I love that old "In the Mood." If you played that song with five guitars our audience would probably go, Wow, what's this!

# PART 2: TALKING BLUES

# GREGG ALLMAN
# (THE ALLMAN BROTHERS BAND)

**JOHN:** Was there something about developing musically in the South that allowed you to form without pressure? In L.A. the business wants you to conform to "what is happening" at the time. If you can develop your sound without outside influences, it's likely you'll be truer to who you are.

**GREGG:** It's not that they are trying to mold you. I think what you are saying is if you are in a place where blues is prevalent, it's a lot easier to get stuff done. I was born in Nashville; my grandmother dragged me down, against my will, to the Auditorium every Saturday night. That old place had church pews; you can't get comfortable in an old hard mahogany church pew. There were rednecks in there throwing whiskey bottles and yelling and screaming. She would say, "I would have you know you saw Hank Williams [Sr.] tonight."

Now they've changed it. Country music has come a long way. This guy Alan Jackson, I like him. But it doesn't compare to Little Milton Campbell, Bobby Bland, Sonny Boy Williamson, and what was born in the Delta.

It's just my own opinion, but this is my formula for rock 'n' roll: Take six parts blues—any kind, Delta, Texas, Chicago, Country-blues, which is like Robert Johnson, Elmore James. Take six parts of that and one part country and you stir it up real good and you give it to a poor white boy and you've got rock 'n' roll.

The way I see it, there's four kings of rock 'n' roll; they are: from Tupelo, Mississippi, Elvis Aaron Presley; from Ferriday, Louisiana, you've got Jerry Lee Lewis; from Macon, Georgia, you've got Little Richard Penniman; and it's not the South but it might as well be, from St. Louis you've got Chuck Berry.

Southern Rock is like saying *rock* rock. We didn't make up that term. That's just a slot, a genre of music that I am proud to say that we had a lot to do with. So, little by little I'm stashing these things away.

Like I figured, every day that passes I think about my beloved brother. Every morning I wake up, I think of him. He had such a passion for music. He quit school in the 10th grade. My brother did three things. He had his arm around a guitar, his arm around a woman, and his head in a book. He used to do my trigonometry homework so we could get to the gig on time.

"It says right here in the book, imbecile." That's what he would call me, imbecile. "It's simple, idiot. If you would put your head in a damn book every now and then it would be a lot easier. It's right there; you've got the answers here; just put them here" [points to his head]. That's called learning it. When it comes test time, you write them down; it's real damn simple." He told me one day, "I bet if they were up there teaching guitar, you would remember it and make straight A's" [laughs]. And he hugged me.

I taught him the basic map of the guitar. He passed me like I was standing still. He quit school immediately and set up night and day. My mother was worried about the both of us. We ate guitar, slept guitar. He would sleep, drink, shower, sweat and shit guitar. We was wrapped around that thing day and night. Sometimes she would make us just put it away.

**JOHN:** Did you have any relationships with the classic blues guys? Did you ever, say, interact with B.B. King? I remember seeing your solo band open for B.B. King at the Ritz in New York.

**GREGG:** I remember that; we did two nights. Other than with the Allman Brothers, that's the first time I ever played on the same bill with B.B. I got a chance to get close, to talk with him. B.B. is like my uncle now. He is my mentor. I learned so much from him.

I could tell you a great story about B.B. He knows that I live in Marin County. I live up by Sonoma, the wine district. It's beautiful. A great place to ride Harley Davidsons. His man, his road/tour manager called my house. B.B. was playing at the Civic Amphitheater, south of Los Angeles. It's down by Disneyland. It's like a Hollywood Bowl–type thing. It's really a nice sounding place.

Anyway, they had this blues review. There was a bunch of people on there. I'm not sure who they had because I was so scared. His man called me and said "the boss," as he referred to him, "would like me to ask you if you would like to come down and play in the Pacific Amphitheater. Come down and play three songs and we'll give you $1,000 a song. B.B. said for me to specify the last three songs."

Man, my heart went into palpitations [laughs]. Don't they know I would have done it for free? Come on. Have you ever heard B.B.'s *Live at the Regal*? You know when you play a record so many times it turns white? I had about three of those. This is when I was in my teens, because that's a pretty old record. But it's like James Brown's *Live at the Apollo*. It's one continuous thing. It's like a medley. He goes from one to another. This is my hero, man, one of them, like Ray [Charles].

So, hell yeah, man, I got out the one Armani jacket I had, threw it in a bag and got on the plane. I got down there and here's what I wanted to know. I wanted to know what three songs and in what key. That's all I wanted to know. That's pretty legit. I couldn't seem to get this information. I called his brother-in–law, the tour manager, and he said you've got to talk to the boss about that.

So, finally, I said, hell. I went down to the gig and I sat there and there's people coming in. I wore a ball cap and tied my hair back, tried to seem inconspicuous. For the first time in my life I actually put on a laminate [backstage pass]. So here comes the big long limousine with the big black bus with the big brass bed in the back. That bus is a killer. Here comes B.B. with his entourage, bodyguard, and whole thing. I came up to him. He said, "Oh, you made it, man." He put his big arms around me, man. I thought I heard one of my ribs crack. He said, "That's great."

I said, "B.B., I've got to know what three songs and in what keys." There were about 25 people around him. He said, "Excuse me, folks. Come here, Gregg." I said, Oh god, what's going to happen now. Am I going to have my ass chewed or what? He takes me in his trailer and says, "You and me do things different in one aspect. Now me, I learned early in the game that a mistake is not the end of the world. If I don't make six mistakes a night it ain't been a good night."

Man, I felt such a weight come off my shoulders. And he says, "You pick the three songs and you call the key." I said all right. And I did. I went out there and I called "Rock Me Baby," the key of F. I called "Stormy Monday Blues," key of G, and then I called one that I had just laid down with the Brothers. Thank goodness I have that big of a repertoire. I could have two songs [laughs].

**JOHN:** How does the gig go with B.B.?

**GREGG:** I got onstage and it went off like clockwork. It was perfect. In other words, at first I thought, Dammit, Gregory, you should have had more faith in this band. The next morning I got up and I was in the mirror shaving and I thought, No man, you should have had more faith in yourself. I learned a whole lot that day. And I'll take it to my grave.

# WALTER BECKER (STEELY DAN)

**WALTER:** I love to play the blues. I'll jam with friends out in the garage. Of course I don't have any friends. Nowadays I play with my drum machine.
**JOHN:** Did you have favorite blues guitarists?
**WALTER:** The usual guys: B.B. King, Hubert Sumlin, Eric Clapton, Otis Rush, of course Jimi Hendrix.

# DICKEY BETTS
# (THE ALLMAN BROTHERS BAND)

**DICKIE:** Duane and Gregg were very strongly urban blues oriented—Ray Charles, B.B. King, Albert King. Gregg's big influence is Bobby "Blue" Bland. Clapton is my all-time favorite. I liked him with Cream. Back during the Jokers, in the early '60s I was doing copy stuff. I was also playing a lot of blues too. I was singing "Stormy Monday" back then. I did a lot of Lonnie Mack stuff. I was going through a real learning process then.

**JOHN:** Who was your favorite artist to sit in with the Allmans?

**DICKIE:** My personal favorite was the first time B.B. King came and jammed with us, because he's an old influence. He is one of my fathers as far as playing guitar. In fact, even as the years went by and the Allman Brothers were a very powerful band, we had B.B. King open shows for us. He would still affect the band to the point where we had trouble playing. We tried to play too clean and too elegant. We jammed with so many people, but B.B. King sticks out.

**JOHN:** Do you still have influences?

**DICKIE:** Yeah. Robert Cray is wonderful to listen too. Stevie Ray Vaughan is an inspiration to hear even though he's heavily influenced by the same songs. For the real thing, you tend to go back to the '30s to really come up with the original inspiration. Robert Johnson, Willie McTell, Lemon Jefferson, the old guys.

# JOE BONAMASSA

**JOHN:** What was your first show-off song. Someone would come over and your mom or dad would say, "Come on, Joe, play for our friend."

**JOE:** You know I never had that. I'm never good on cue. I'm really bad at "Okay play, okay practice." Today we live in a very sound-bite time. Pack it all in 15 seconds and put it on Instagram. Give me a few seconds to figure this out. That was my trick; I would jam along. I had a little tape deck. It was a little distorted, but it was just loud enough I could play the cassette.

I had a Silvertone [Model] 1482 amp, which had a single 12-inch [speaker]. And if you turned it all the way up, it sounded like a half-stack Marshall Bluesbreaker or [Fender] Deluxe, like a [Fender] Brown. It wasn't very loud but it was just loud enough where I could jam along with a Cream record. I'd jam along with Robben Ford or I'd jam along with Eric Johnson and B.B. King. All these big jump blues records. There was some Jeff Beck Group.

And my parents started to realize I was pretty good. They couldn't tell the difference between my solos and Eric Clapton because I was able to mimic the sound and kind of join in. I'd play rhythm, I'd play lead. I knew the whole thing. And they were like, You really want to do this. I'm about eight years old at the time. I say yeah.

I had been playing five or six years and I remember the fourth grade music class learned how to play guitar. My music teacher at the school asked if anybody knew how to play guitar. Nobody raised their hands. I begrudgingly raised my hand.

"Would you like to play for the class?"

That was a nightmare for me because I was a very shy kid. I said okay and I got up and played. I started doing this bluegrass thing I learned. And I see the music teacher run out of the room, grab the principal and the high school music teacher, and before you know it I'm in the principal's office.

"How long have you been playing?"

I said, "Oh, about six years."

"How come we didn't know this?"

"I play at home."

"Why didn't you sign up to join the school band?"

I go, "Because I don't wanna play Dixieland shit, I want to play blues."

They called my parents. "Do you know he plays guitar extraordinarily well for his age?"

"Oh yeah, he's been playing forever."

I kept it so underground. That was my life. When I got home, I did my homework. I did what I was supposed to do. But when all that was over, I grabbed my copy of Tom Wheeler's *American Guitars* book, looked through pages of vintage guitars and I would jam along with records and that was the DNA of it all.

# GILBY CLARKE (GUNS N' ROSES)

**GILBY:** There is nothing more simplistic than the blues. How do you rewrite those same three chords. Rod Stewart does a great job. I love the blues and it's great to hear what a band like the [Black] Crowes did with, say, "Hard to Handle." It's awesome. It's a great song but what they did with it is a nice way to move it along.

Guitar playing back then was pretty much blues-based, but the British stuff stuck a little closer to the blues. I think the American stuff is a little more riff-oriented. An English band would take the I-IV-V and play it and add some stuff, where the Americans like Ted Nugent would have some really great riffs. That's the difference between Slash and me. Slash would write a song around a riff, where I would write a song around a chord.

## WILLIE DIXON

**JOHN:** Is there a blues writing style?

**WILLIE:** My parents used to tell me most people thought the blues was just something that somebody would be hollering and it didn't mean very much. They explained to me why these people were hollering like this, raising hell one way or the other, whether it was good or bad, past or present. They would express the facts of life through their feeling of the music.

At the time when they first started, the people that made the blues were the slaves. They had to talk around the boss man to deliver their message to each other without letting him know. This is why they used so many slangs in the various things they created. By using this it gave them a chance to let each other know about how they felt about various things. They began to communicate to each other right under the boss's nose. This is the way the style developed.

**JOHN:** Is that the reason for saying a line, repeating it and then giving the punch line?

**WILLIE:** Well, you see, that was to get attention. That was the main thing because if someone has their mind on something else, you'd say something the first time and they wouldn't be aware of what was happening. After you wait a little longer and you think you've got their attention, you'd say the same thing again. You wait even longer and you know they're listening and then all of a sudden here comes the punch line. In between the particular statement you made in the first place, you would let time lapse and go into other conversations about everything else. Then all of a sudden here comes the punch line and nobody thought anything of it but the one you were communicating with.

**JOHN:** Do you have any favorite performance of your tunes as recorded by Cream, Led Zeppelin, the Allman Brothers, or Albert King?

**WILLIE:** I'm happy with all of them because it gives it a much better chance to be properly exposed. If you can't get exposed by water, then you take it by land to the same place and it's just as good.

**JOHN:** I mean performance-wise. For example, "I'm Ready" has been recorded by a lot of different artists with different arrangements.

**WILLIE:** Performance-wise I like 'em all because this is what the blues is all about. The blues is the basic. The people use all these basics to do whatever they do. Like when they made the first automobile, it was probably like the wagon. It didn't have a motor—the horse was the motor. Then they made the motor and the next guy put the windshield wipers on. The next added lights. They kept adding to it. The blues is the basic and everything in American music has been built onto this basic of the blues. But the majority of people don't look at that. Just like when you look at the automobile of today, and then you look at that model they built at first, you don't believe it's the same thing. They call it the same thing but it's a different thing. It's the same with music, the basics remain the same.

# JIMI HENDRIX

**JIMI:** The first guitarist I was very aware of was Muddy Waters. I heard one of his records when I was a little boy and it scared me to death. I heard all those sounds. Wow, what was *that* all about? I'd go out to the back porch there in Seattle, and I'd play guitar to a Muddy Waters record. I liked Muddy Waters when he had two guitars, harmonica and bass drum. Things like "Rollin' Stone" and "Rollin' and Tumblin' " were what I liked, that real primitive guitar sound. I was trying to learn how to play like Chuck Berry and Muddy Waters. I dug Howlin' Wolf and Elmore James. Robert Johnson, he's so cool.

There was other stuff, too: Richie Valens, Eddie Cochran's "Summertime Blues." Chet Atkins, Jimmy Reed. When I first started, I liked anything from B.B. King to Bach. Those were just the people that gave me the feeling to get my own thing together. Most of the guitarists came from the South. There's one cat I'm still trying to get across to people. His name is Albert Collins; he's a very smooth guitarist who plays around Texas. He's buried in a road band somewhere. He's good, really good. But he's a family cat and doesn't want to go too far from home. Ain't that always the way? And Albert King, he plays completely and strictly in one way, just straight funk blues, very funky sound, which is great; one of the funkiest I've heard. These are some of the best guitarists in the world.

Blues is part of America. It means Elmore James and Howlin'

Wolf and Robert Johnson. It means Muddy Waters and Bo Diddley. Now someone is going to laugh about Bo Diddley being in there, but if you want the backbone of the real pioneering thing which Clapton and others are into, that's it. I like Bo Diddley a lot. Bo made a great contribution to rock. Everybody has some blues to offer. Color just doesn't make a difference. My main thing is the blues.

# ALBERT KING

**JOHN:** When you first learned guitar, did you figure out the chords or did someone show you?
**ALBERT:** I figured it out; I played by ear all of those years until 1967, '68. Then I went to a music school at night to learn how to arrange and voice. Most naturally within that I learned theory and my chord changes. I know now I could make some of them, but many chords I didn't know about but I knew my keys; I could play in any key on the board.
**JOHN:** Did you learn single notes by what sounded right as opposed to patterns?
**ALBERT:** Something I felt, so I won't get rid of that; I'll keep that till I die. It's my style.
**JOHN:** Did you ever try to impersonate another player?
**ALBERT:** Many people. I can play like anybody in the South, but they can't play like me. This was the only way that I could play and make music 'cause I didn't have any records out. So I had to play what you had recorded or what the people like. You put out something funky and I would cut it. Every time a hot tune would come as a vocal, I would do the instrumental, so I figured that was smart. I had to learn how to play like anybody from rock 'n' roll to Ray Charles to Count Basie; we played it all.
**JOHN:** I read your first guitar you took a wire and attached it to your house?
**ALBERT:** Well, that was a sound wire. I nailed a wire on the side

of the wall. Back in those days they made those twist brooms with bitty steel wire, and so I nailed it to the side of the wall, put a bottle at the top and a brick at the bottom. I was playing bottleneck long before Elmore James. I was a little boy.

**JOHN:** You named your guitar Lucy. What is that about?

**ALBERT:** Well, I named my guitar Lucy when I recorded that record "I Love Lucy."

**JOHN:** From the TV show?

**ALBERT:** Yes, Lucille Ball, that's my favorite lady. And I recorded a tune about *I Love Lucy* so I named my guitar Lucy. Then later B.B. named his guitar Lucille. And if you look on the head of mine it says Lucy. I've got the first Flying V made, the very first one.

**JOHN:** How do you feel knowing you have influenced so many other great players and they have reaped the money and you have not?

**ALBERT:** Well, they can't play like me. I haven't run across a man yet could play like me. So, whatever they do to make their bucks would be on their own playing. There's one thing: you can go out for a while playing like the next man, but you've got to change and do your own thing sooner or later.

**JOHN:** Did you stop listening to other players in order to do that?

**ALBERT:** Yes, I listened to other players and I listened to their mistakes. I tried to play the next man's mistakes. It's been a long hard scuffle, but it's okay.

# B.B. KING

**JOHN:** I heard your first musical experiences were growing up in Indianola.

**B.B.:** When you come up as I did, my mother was into gospel music. The sanctified church they would go to, the preacher played guitar. When I got to know anybody other than my mom, I was listening to music. I don't really know when it started. When I was about eight or nine it sounded so good to me. I just wanted to play.

The preacher was the brother-in-law to my uncle. When I would visit my uncle's house, the preacher would come visit his sister and my uncle and have dinner on Sunday evening. In the South, when I was growing up, most of the times if you were a kid you had to wait until after the adults had finished eating. The adults would be eating and we kids would be outside or in the living room playing. Usually the preacher would lay his guitar on the bed and that's how I'd get ahold of it. I was maybe ten years old.

One day he caught me; I felt sure he would really get on me about it. My uncle kind of scolded me, but the preacher said, "Don't scold him," and he showed me three chords—I IV V—and I've been playing them ever since. That's my music lesson, and from that time on I never had anybody actually teach me.

**JOHN:** Did you listen to Big Bill Broonzy?

**B.B.:** I did listen to Big Bill Broonzy and I liked him, but he was not my idol. My idol was Lonnie Johnson and Blind Lemon. I heard Robert Johnson and Big Bill Broonzy. But for guitar, Lonnie

Johnson and Blind Lemon Jefferson were blues. When I started to hearing Charlie Christian and Django Reinhardt and jazz, that did it.

At [house] parties in early 1939 or '40 I heard T-Bone Walker on electric guitar playing single-string blues and I went crazy. When he did "Stormy Monday" in '42 or '43, I'd just been drafted in the army. I was 18 in '43. I had heard of him and heard him, but when I heard "Stormy Monday," that's the one that did it. Ever since then, it seemed to me, combining Blind Lemon, Lonnie Johnson, and T-Bone Walker. I could somehow hear a cohesiveness, if you will, between the blues and jazz and gospel on the guitar. I could hear some of it all intertwined.

Then I also listened to other people on other instruments, like Louis Jordan, Johnny Hodges on alto sax, Bobby Hackett on trumpet. Somehow the way they phrase is like a sword that seems to go right straight through. Just a few people can do that to me. They don't be playing a lot of notes, and it's kind of like I've watched on TV, when people like Ella Fitzgerald break the glass. You may look at that a little weird, but it is a certain something and some of those notes when it hits me, it pierces right straight through. It will make me stop doing whatever I'm doing and listen. That's what I mean.

**JOHN:** Dizzy Gillespie told a story where the band was swinging so hard and sounding so good he ran out of the club because it freaked him out.

**B.B.:** It's very powerful because it's been many times you get things and you don't know what to do with them; it's heaven.

**JOHN:** You were talking about how it is that makes these few people put it together in a certain way. What you do, you can hear all the different influences—a trumpet riff, sax, T-Bone, every note is so full of life. When that happens, it doesn't matter what instrument it is.

**B.B.:** I thank you, man; at least somebody is being able to understand my feelings. When you're doing it, I'm sure, as a musician yourself, you really try to put it together in your own head as you play. That's what happens to me. I want my audience of one or 100 to enjoy what I'm doing. I want them to feel it. There are times there's just nobody there but me. I'm into what I'm doing. It's almost like the spirit leaves the body and gets into what I'm doing. After a while it comes back and says, I sure hope you enjoyed it because I had a ball.

There are many other times when you can't seem to put it together. I've had many nights like that; even though I'll hit a note, it's never a time when I don't enjoy some of what I'm doing. There are many times it's like trying to tell a story and your punch line comes out before the rest of the story. Many nights many good musicians like yourself paint beautiful pictures; some of us just walk down the path of playing and there ain't no grass or trees or ladies or birds. We just go through it. There are others as they go down the path of playing; they paint you a beautiful picture, a little lake here or a creek there. People are on the other side of the creek fishing. There's a car on a road but I'm on the path and wheat is over there. Some guys seem to do it every time.

There is another part of my career which I don't think was recorded. I used to think in terms of speed versus economy, I would take speed. Today it's always economy. I'd rather just ration the notes.

**JOHN:** Space, where to hit it. There is only one B.B. King, but the thing about the blues that is fascinating is where to hold back, the tension and release. You never know. I feel that you don't know exactly. When your instinct and your intellect get together between hanging back and leaving space or suddenly rushing in with notes, that is something you do like nobody else.

**B.B.:** Thank you very much. I've played with some of the jazz players, some of the gospel players, some of the rock players. If I don't know the chords, I've learned to trail along and play common tones in the chords. As they played the beautiful chords, I'll hold a common tone that leads from one chord to the other. What

I'm trying to say to you is knowing that you only have three chord changes in most of the 12-bar blues, you've got to be kind of like a woman who knows many tricks about making love. You can't stay with the one and let it be dead. You've got to find something to color each passage that leads to the next chord.

Think about it: you've got four bars before you make a change. Then when you go and feel IV, that's when you've got to try to do something there before you get back to your tonic chord again. If you're playing any of the standards, like "Body and Soul," it modulates to another key when you get into the bridge. Any of those standard tunes, you can play a chord on every beat if you wanted to. If your vocab is happening, it can make it work. I hear a lot of people do it when it's not working, to me, but they still can do it.

**JOHN:** Why do you think blues continues generation after generation?

**B.B.:** I think blues doesn't put on airs; it's just, this is it. You see what you get. It's not a highfalutin type of music. It's down to earth. It's just like kids. If you ask a kid something, they tell you the truth; you've got to make them lie. Blues music is usually just that truth. It's down-home music. It's not like talking to a college professor.

It's the type of music that everybody can understand. There are parts of it that are sophisticated, but the sophisticated part of it sits right in there among the simple parts. If one like yourself and many other learned people know, they are the ones able to pick it out. Other people that are not learned and just like a good sound and feel, it's good for them too.

It's good for whatever ails you. That's one of the things that made it stay around so long and has been like food to people that need it. My last statement is, blues to me is like a mother tree. Many branches of music have sprouted from it. The tree didn't stop growing, but there are many branches all over. A few of us that didn't graduate, we had to stay with it.

## ANDREAS KISSER (SEPULTURA)

**ANDREAS:** I like Stevie Ray Vaughan because he plays the blues in all different ways and not always the same, like B.B. King. He is a more aggressive guitar player. I had a chance to see him live in '89 in Philadelphia with Jeff Beck opening for him. It was great. I love to play blues all the time. I listen to Stevie Ray Vaughan and Gatemouth Brown. He is killer.
**JOHN:** Does it influence your music?
**ANDREAS:** Yeah, everything is an influence. Not directly. You cannot pick up a Sepulture album and hear a blues lick or a classical lick, but it's there for sure.

# JONNY LANG

**JOHN:** Can you remember your first lessons?

**JONNY:** Yeah, we started with the 12-bar blues, bending notes and vibrato. My teacher, Ted Larsen, showed me what to do, but what helped me most was that he turned me onto really good music, and I went home and studied that. He gave me one of his Albert King albums (*Live Wire Blues Power*). I loved it right away.

**JOHN:** What other records did you wear out?

**JONNY:** Stevie Ray Vaughan's *Couldn't Stand the Weather* and Albert Collins' *Ice Pickin'*. I was just trying to play along with the records and learn some licks from them. I wasn't really trying to imitate them. Maybe a month after I started, I was able to kind of play along with songs. I just learned the scales, but I am not technical at all. I don't know what I'm playing half the time. I'm not saying that I don't know anything technically. I don't know stuff Eric Johnson knows.

**JOHN:** Do you relate your phrasing as a vocalist to your phrasing as a guitarist?

**JONNY:** The two definitely go hand in hand. I have different influences for singing than I do for guitar playing. For singing there's Stevie Wonder and Otis Redding and B.B. King. I like their phrasing and the way they put stuff in the song. Albert Collins and B.B. King are my favorite guitar players.

## ALVIN LEE (TEN YEARS AFTER)

**JOHN:** What was you take on the British Blues Explosion in the 1960s.

**ALVIN:** John Mayall started the blues boom in England in the 1960s. We were going around making a living playing. You had to kind of do a bit of what was in the charts to play in dance halls, and which is a bit like working for a living. Then suddenly the blues boom happened.

I was brought up on the blues. My father used to collect "ethnic chain gang" songs and stuff like that, and suddenly the blues was the thing to be doing. So suddenly I had this great repertoire, and I could put all these songs in. It was like a breath of freedom, to suddenly to say the blues was hip, and before it wasn't.

I think we've got John Mayall to thank for that. When we first came to America they called it "The English sound," and we were playing what we thought was American. We were playing American music. What I used to hate about the blues thing was these blues "purists" that used to come to gigs and say, "You played that B.B. King song wrong, because you didn't play those notes exactly like he did."

I just used to go for the feel and emulate the feel. I never used to copy notes. A lot of guitarists will copy things note for note. I don't think that does you any good, 'cause you don't develop your own style. There's a lot of good guitarists that can play everyone else's solos note for note, but they haven't really got their own thing going for them. That used to annoy the hell out of me, people saying, "That wasn't a proper Elmore James version 'cause you did it wrong." How can you do a blues song wrong? You're gonna copy the guy's original mistakes, and then it's right? I used to kick against that, you know. My idea was, I'd just play my version of B.B. King, or my version of Elmore James.

# JOHN MAYALL

**JOHN S.:** What is the common element your guitarists have?
**JOHN M.:** This intensity of what they put into one note. Like B.B. King will play one note and it will sing and have a purity about it that says so much. If any guitar player has that kind of thing in him—that feel that comes across in the course of one note—then you know you're on the right track.
**JOHN S.:** Has the blues intrinsically changed at all since the late '50s and early '60s?
**JOHN M.:** The heart of it never changes, but I think the sound of it does change. It's always managed to be contemporary music whatever year something comes out. It always reflects the life and times of where it came from. To me the blues is a wonderful form because it is probably the only music that actually does that. Each one can actually be like a short movie.

I see pictures when I hear the music. Consequently, something that was recorded back in 1929 in the Mississippi Delta will give you a picture of what that must have been like. It puts you in a place and time and social situation. An uptown Chicago blues thing will give you a picture of the city. I think the blues is finding its way into so many different kinds of contemporary music. You'd have to have a longer discussion than this to try and carve it all up, but we do feel it. At least 50 percent of the rock music you hear comes from the blues. The same with jazz too. Blues and jazz are roots American music. They will always be with us.

**JOHN S.:** You and Paul Butterfield, Art Blakey and Miles Davis are considered schools because of the many musical giants who graduated from your bands. Were you aware of that, or is it a label we put on you?
**JOHN M.:** It's one of those things that stuck because people have chosen to label it that way. It's true to a certain extent. It's not a school where we're all working musicians. As a bandleader, the bandleader always gives the direction and is responsible for what comes out on the overall thing. I've always thought of myself as a bandleader, not a schoolteacher. I didn't say this is the way it goes. All I could do was turn people onto certain records and say, Check this out, and whatever influences they got would be fine.

In the case of Eric Clapton, who was the first person who I ever worked with to have that kind of affinity for the blues, he had the natural feel for it. He was unique in England at that time. He remains to this day a unique guitar player.

# KEB' MO'

**JOHN:** How did the *Keb' Mo'* record happen?
**KEB':** I started the ball myself. I didn't wait on a record company. I felt like I didn't need a record company. I proceeded with the feeling that I wanted to put the music out there and I wasn't going to wait on anybody to do it for me. So every time I got a few extra bucks I'd go and record something in the studio solo. 1 didn't have to call musicians. I just did it solo. I started by actually selling tapes at the club. I put eight songs on a tape. A lot of them are on this *[Keb' Mo']* record. The response was really good. I was selling here locally [L.A.] and I started hearing from people on the East Coast that somehow got this tape and were playing it. I gave a copy of it to my producer, John Porter [Buddy Guy, Taj Mahal, Roxy Music, the Smiths]. I didn't even know him, I just met him. He brought me to Sony and hooked it up from one of those tapes I gave him.
**JOHN:** This sounds like you recorded live.
**KEB':** That's how I recorded it. That's how you record when you've got your own money in your pocket. The guy said, "Okay, the studio cost $30 an hour." You got $60 bucks. You've got to get it down in a couple hours. All of the songs were rerecorded, but "Every Morning" is from when I went into the studio and did it on my own. That's the version I had on my cassette. I liked that version so much, why bother doing it again?

## GARY MOORE

**JOHN:** Didn't you start as a blues player?

**GARY:** The first few years of my playing were devoted to the blues. It was more sort of the British blues than the ethnic blues of America. I was into the guitar aspect of the blues. I was heavily into early Clapton and that sort of thing. I think the *Bluesbreakers* album turned a lot of guitar players around, at least in England. That album with Clapton was probably the one album that revolutionized guitar playing around the world. I was 14 when all that came out, but I'd been playing since I was 10 or 11. I'd been through the Shadows sort of thing. That was the big deal when I was a kid.

**JOHN:** Was Clapton your hero?

**GARY:** I really liked Peter Green. I was more into the feeling and the emotion of his playing. I found it very pure. I found it very appealing that he wasn't a flash player, yet I found the emotional content of his playing to be very intense. I emulated him, I suppose. He's still one of my main influences.

**JOHN:** Was there a particular record of his that you got off on?

**GARY:** I liked his work with John Mayall on *Hard Road*. In fact, the guitar that I play now is the guitar Green used on that album. He sold it to me about nine years ago.

**JOHN:** Bernie Marsden [Whitesnake] has Clapton's guitar from the *Bluesbreakers* album.

**GARY:** That's not true. A lot of people make claims to having that guitar, but nobody really knows who has it. He's got one of Eric's guitars, but it isn't the one from the *Bluesbreakers* album. I know mine is real because I bought it directly from Peter Green. It's the one he bought in 1967. It's also the one from all the early Fleetwood Mac albums.

**JOHN:** Why did he sell it?

**GARY:** When he went through that emotional and difficult period after he left Fleetwood Mac, he wanted to get rid of all his possessions. It was due to him that I was in England in the first place. Skid Row [Gary's Irish band] had opened for Fleetwood Mac in Ireland. Peter was one of my big heroes and he really liked my guitar playing a lot. He suggested to his manager at the time, Clifford Davis, that he sign us up and bring us over to England. So, he really gave me my first big break. It was nice for mc because he was such a big hero of mine. To have him turn around and admire what I was doing, and also help me, was just the greatest compliment.

# PAUL RODGERS
# (FREE, BAD COMPANY, THE FIRM)

**JOHN:** Have we progressed since Muddy Waters? Have we added to the blues, or embellished what has been?

**PAUL:** Technically we have definitely advanced. The sounds today are just wonderful. There's a fabulous drum sound available and a great range of color is available through synthesizers. But I think we have drifted away from what the essence of the blues is. I wish I could say what the essence of the blues is, but I guess to my interpretation it is a thing from inside, a mood. It's an expression of an emotion rather than a demonstration of ability. You don't have to be brilliant to say something.

**JOHN:** Was Bad Company a blues band using that criteria?

**PAUL:** I don't think that Bad Company was a blues band, although having said that I think almost all rock 'n' roll is somewhat blues-based.

**JOHN:** Where does blues turn into rock 'n' roll?

**PAUL:** [Whistles] Wow! What an interesting thing, because one of the ideas when Phil Carson called me and we spoke about doing a blues album, he got the idea from something Jimmy Page and I did with the Firm, which was a Muddy Waters song called "I Just Want to Make Love to You." I guess what we did was take a blues song and give it a rock 'n' roll treatment—whatever that is. I guess what that is, is to electrify it and give it a sort of wall of sound thing. I don't know if it's an improvement; it's just a reinterpretation in our style.

# RICHIE SAMBORA (BON JOVI)

**JOHN:** In your mind, Stevie Wonder, Led Zeppelin and Muddy Waters are all related.

**RICHIE:** Absolutely, there is a big parallel. Jimmy Page feels the same way. Any kind of Delta blues music going back to, say, "I'm a Man" by Muddy Waters, is all the same vibe. What Jimmy Page did was make those things a little complex and Stevie Wonder took those simplistic things he knew and listened to as a kid and brought them into "Signed, Sealed, Delivered." That has the same rhythmic quality in the music. Basically, it's rhythm guitar but it's played as a melody. Just like "Lay Your Hands on Me" could be a horn line but it's played with rhythm guitar. It's only the application of it that makes it Bon Jovi and rock 'n' roll. It could be anything.

# NEAL SCHON (JOURNEY)

**NEAL:** If you can feel the hurt, you can play the blues. My roots are definitely black blues. I spent years of my life with this band [Journey] trying to play guitar. And just playing a blues solo ["Dock of the Bay" with Michael Bolton], everybody goes, Wow.

## PAT SIMMONS (THE DOOBIE BROTHERS)

**PAT:** I was taking guitar lessons and the lady that gave me lessons had all these records and I would listen to them. I started listening to country and blues and particularly Doc Watson, the Reverend Gary Davis and Lightnin' Hopkins. Then I heard Jorma Kaukonen. He used to play around San Jose. I thought, Man, this is it. This guy has reached the pinnacle of what I want to do. I want to be a country/blues–based kind of guitar player and I want to sing the blues.

**JOHN:** Who brought you to the electric guitar?

**PAT:** Jorma, when he started playing with the Airplane. It wasn't just Jorma. My favorite band of that era was Paul Butterfield. Mike Bloomfield became the epitome of the guitar player. I bought every Paul Butterfield album. I listened to every record. I copied as much as I could from Mike Bloomfield. I think he really brought me into it. Then from Mike Bloomfield, the city blues; Chicago blues became so much the thing for me. From there it was B.B. King, Albert King, Freddie King, all the Kings. I never heard guitar playing like that. Jimi Hendrix took it one step further from what I had been listening too. For me, B.B. King and Mike Bloomfield were the two that really turned me on to guitar.

## EDDIE VAN HALEN (VAN HALEN)

**JOHN:** Did you study the blues?

**EDDIE:** I didn't really study it. When I first started soloing, those were just the simplest, easiest notes to hit. When I stumbled into it, I said, Hey, this is what they're doing in the blues. I said, Shit, I know those notes. Great. And I just kind of expanded from there.

# PART 3: A SELECTIVE DISCOGRAPHY

# A SELECTIVE DISCOGRAPHY

The following recordings were either mentioned in a positive way or recommended by:

**Gregg Allman**
*Live at the Regal* / B.B. King

**Paul Barrere**
*Keb' Mo'*

**Jason Becker**
*The Last Waltz* / The Band

**Dickey Betts**
*The Best of Blind Lemon Jefferson*
*The Best of Blind Willie McTell*
*The Best of Robert Johnson*

**Vito Bratta**
*Couldn't Stand the Weather* / Stevie Ray Vaughan
*Soul to Soul* / Stevie Ray Vaughan
*Texas Flood* / Stevie Ray Vaughan

**Robert Cray**
*Greatest Hits* / Tyrone Davis

**Warren DeMartini**
*Roots Revisted* / Maceo Parker
*Sticky Fingers* / The Rolling Stones

**Robben Ford**
*Just Before the Bullets Fly* / Gregg Allman
*A Long Time Comin'* / The Electric Flag
*Miles in the Sky* / Miles Davis
*Miles Smiles* / Miles Davis
*Nefertiti* / Miles Davis
*Sorcerer* / Miles Davis

**David Gilmour**
*Alchemy: Dire Straits Live*

**Buddy Guy**
*Ledbetter Heights* / Kenny Wayne Shepherd

**Warren Haynes**
*Schizophonic* / Robben Ford

**Eric Johnson**
*Are You Experienced* / The Jimi Hendrix Experience
*Axis: Bold As Love* / The Jimi Hendrix Experience
*Blues Breakers with Eric Clapton* / John Mayall
*Disraeli Gears* / Cream
*Electric Ladyland* / The Jimi Hendrix Experience
*Super Session* / Al Kooper (with Mike Bloomfield)
*Truth* / Jeff Beck
*Wheels of Fire* / Cream

**Jonny Lang**
*Couldn't Stand the Weather* / Stevie Ray Vaughan
*Ice Pickin'* / Albert Collins
*Live Wire Blues Power* / Albert King

**Alex Lifeson**
*Crusade* / John Mayall & the Bluesbreakers

**George Lynch**
*ZZ Top's First Album*

**Brian May**
*The Paul Butterfield Blues Band*

**Gary Moore**
*Blues Breakers with Eric Clapton* / John Mayall
*Hard Road* / John Mayall & the Bluesbreakers

**Dave Murray**
*Texas Flood* / Stevie Ray Vaughan
*Theme* / Leslie West

**Dave Sanborn**
*From the Heart* / Hank Crawford

**Kenny Wayne Shepherd**
*In Step* / Stevie Ray Vaughan
*Live Wire Blues Power* / Albert King

**Pat Simmons**
*East-West* / The Butterfield Blues Band
*The Paul Butterfield Blues Band*

**Jimmy Vaughan**

*The Wham of That Memphis Man* / Lonnie Mack

**Johnny Winter**

*The Best of Little Walter*
*The Best of Muddy Waters*
*The Best of Robert Johnson, Vol. I and II*
*The Best of Sonny Boy Williamson*
*Bop Till You Drop* / Ry Cooder
*Born Under a Bad Sign* / Albert King
*Singin' the Blues* / B.B. King

www.ingramcontent.com/pod-product-compliance
Ingram Content Group UK Ltd.
Pitfield, Milton Keynes, MK11 3LW, UK
UKHW021907190726
13853UKWH00002B/562

9 798460 127221